CityPack
Munich

TERESA FISHER

Teresa Fisher is a freelance travel writer who lived in Munich for five years. Having returned to England, she continues to contribute to a number of newspapers and German magazines, including a monthly travel column in Munich Found. *She has also written a variety of travel books on France.*

D1486567

City-centre map continues on inside back cover

AA Publishing

Contents

About this book

KEY TO SYMBOLS

✚	map reference on the fold-out map accompanying this book (see below)	🚌	nearest bus route
✉	address	⛴	nearest riverboat or ferry stop
☎	telephone number	♿	facilities for visitors with disabilities
🕐	opening times	✋	admission charge
🍴	restaurant or café on premises or nearby	⬌	other nearby places of interest
Ⓜ	nearest Metro (underground) train station	❓	tours, lectures, or special events
🚆	nearest overground train station	➤	indicates the page where you will find a fuller description
		ℹ	tourist infomation

CityPack Munich is divided into six sections to cover the six most important aspects of your visit to Munich. It includes:

- The author's view of the city and its people
- Itineraries, walks and excursions
- The top 25 sights to visit – as selected by the author
- Features about different aspects of the city that make it special
- Detailed listings of restaurants, hotels, shops and nightlife
- Practical information

In addition, easy-to-read side panels provide fascinating extra facts and snippets, highlights of places to visit and invaluable practical advice.

CROSS-REFERENCES

To help you make the most of your visit, cross-references, indicated by ➤ , show you where to find additional information about a place or subject.

MAPS

- **The fold-out map** in the wallet at the back of the book is a comprehensive street plan of Munich. All the map references given in the book refer to this map. For example, the BMW-Museum on Petuelring 130 has the following information: ✚ J22 – indicating the grid square of the map in which the BMW-Museum will be found.
- **The city-centre maps** found on the inside front and back covers of the book itself are for quick reference. They show the Top 25 Sights, described on pages 24–48, which are clearly plotted by number (❶ – ㉕, not page number) from west to east across the city.

PRICES

Where appropriate, an indication of the cost of an establishment is given by **£** signs: **£££** denotes higher prices, **££** denotes average prices, while **£** denotes lower charges.

MUNICH
life

A PERSONAL VIEW

The Glockenspiel,
New Town Hall

'What is Munich all about?' The question once posed by artist Kurt Schwitters apparently has no answer. Yet surveys show that it is Germany's most popular city and that, given the choice, over half the German population would choose to live in Munich, the capital of Bavaria. Those who live here claim that it is more than just an exceptionally attractive city. It radiates a unique atmosphere that is hard to define although many have tried: 'village of a million', 'metropolis with a heart', 'Athens on the Isar', even 'the secret capital of Germany'. The list of epithets goes on ...

To understand Munich, you really need to understand the Bavarian people. It is their smug patriotism and deep-rooted conservatism which underpins the city, creating a rare balance of German urban efficiency and rural Alpine romanticism. The best time to visit is spring or summer; long hazy months when even the blue skies with their fleecy white clouds mirror the Free State's 'national' colours. Look closely and you will see that blue and white diamonds dominate every aspect of Munich life, from the BMW logo to the livery of its famous breweries.

The clichéd image many have of a 'typical' German is actually a Bavarian, sporting leather shorts, feasting on sausage and dumplings, and accompanied by a *Dirndl*-clad lady armed with at least a dozen huge mugs of beer (27 is the current record!). For here, *Lederhosen* and felt hats with tufts resembling shaving brushes are *de rigueur* – part of a cherished centuries-old folk tradition – and an outward proclamation of their proud individuality. Don't worry if you can't understand the dialect – most Germans have the same problem.

'Green' Munich

Munich is ideally located less than an hour from the Alps and a stone's throw from Austria, Italy and Switzerland, so at the weekends, there is always a mass exodus to the villages, lakes and mountains whatever the season. Summer, however, belongs to Munich's English Garden, and the River Isar, with activities ranging from beach barbecues to nude sunbathing, is more alive than any other city river in the world.

Native-born Münchners are a rarity. The majority of inhabitants come from other parts of Germany, although they all regard themselves as citizens of Munich in spirit. Nearly a quarter of the population is foreign, giving Munich a truly international flavour. The city's social scene is fast and fun, with a thriving student population crammed into the bars and cafés of trendy Schwabing, but it is in the old town centre around Marienplatz where the city's heart beats loudest. Munich is a city of writers, artists, musicians and film-makers, the rich and the jet-set, who cruise the boulevards in their Porsche convertibles.

Take the U-Bahn (underground) at 6AM and you will find a lot of sleepy-looking people going to work. These are your average Münchners: diligent, efficient, dedicated to their work but even more dedicated to their *Freizeit* (free time). Perhaps it is the close proximity to Italy which causes lunch hours to get longer and the working day to get shorter? Come 3PM many are back on the tube, and heading for the city's legendary beer gardens, as the Münchners' real joy is to drink a cool beer in the shade of chestnut trees in the English Garden. The jovial

A mystery wind

Munich's continental climate guarantees icy winters and hot summers, but there is also the famous *Föhn* wind, which can strike at any time of year. This warm, dry, Alpine wind guarantees amazing crystal-clear views (the Alps seem almost close enough to touch), but it is also blamed for headaches and bad moods. So if drivers seem more wreckless, barmaids more short-tempered and the locals blunter than usual, perhaps it's the *Föhn!*

Enjoying a beer in the English Garden

Munich life

'How can one speak of Munich but to say it is a kind of German heaven? Some people sleep and dream they are in paradise, but all over Germany people sometimes dream they have gone to Munich.' Thomas Wolfe, 1925

'Don't bother going anywhere else ... nothing can match Munich. Everything else in Germany is a waste of time.' Ernest Hemingway, 1923

Musician from an oom-pah band

atmosphere of the beer gardens, where social distinctions cease to matter, brings out the best in everyone: the Bavarian *joie de vivre*, a passion for outdoor life, sociability and an infectious determination to enjoy. Don't be surprised if a stranger suddenly links arms with you to sway to the music of an oom-pah band.

Beer plays an unashamedly important role in Munich life. Where else in the world is drinking considered the main activity for weeks at a stretch, and its beer festivals counted as 'seasons'? Munich's breweries also play a significant economic role, alongside a thriving service industry. After Frankfurt, Munich is Germany's largest banking centre, headquarters of the country's insurance sector, a leading centre of fashion and film-making, the world's second publishing and media city after New York, and Germany's second-largest industrial city. It also has a reputation as Germany's most expensive city, with spiralling rents and expensive public transport making the cost of living beyond the reach of many people.

We cannot ignore the Bavarian capital's close associations with the rise of Nazism. However, we can be grateful that after World War II, although half its buildings were reduced to rubble, unlike so many German cities it chose to restore and reconstruct the great palaces and churches of its past, re-creating one of Europe's most beautiful cities with its historic buildings, handsome parks and world-class museums, galleries and theatres.

So what *is* Munich all about? A village of a million or a bustling metropolis? A mixture of central European efficiency and Mediterranean atmosphere, of BMW and the bohemian, of technology and tradition, or just a *gemütlich*, good-time city? Come and find out for yourself.

MUNICH IN FIGURES

A welcoming sign

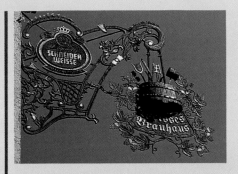

PEOPLE

- Population (1995): 1,324,000 (including 280,000 foreigners)
- Historical growth: 1846 – 100,000 inhabitants; 1939 – 829,000; 1945 – 480,000; 1957 – 1,000,000
- Religion: 56 per cent Roman Catholic; 20 per cent Protestant
- Number of students at Munich University (Germany's largest): 102,807
- Estimated number of tourists annually: 50 million day-visitors; 6 million overnight stays

LEISURE

- Munich has 83 cinemas, 53 bookshops, 53 museums, 48 theatres, 3 symphony orchestras
- Number of sports clubs: 800
- Area of parkland: 4,181 hectares
- Number of bicycle owners: 25,000
- Cycle paths: 1,300km

GEOGRAPHY

- Area of city: 310sq km
- Number of districts: 41
- Annual temperature range: -5°C to 32°C
- Annual hours of sunshine: 1,748
- Distance from Alps: 50km

BEER

- Number of breweries: 7
- Annual production: 400 million litres
- Annual turnover: DM1.2 billion
- Münchners are the world's largest consumers of beer, downing an annual 190 litres per head

9

A Chronology

777	First recorded mention of Munichen ('the home of monks').
1158	Henry the Lion founds the city of Munich.
1180	Bavaria becomes the territory of the Wittelsbach rulers.
1327	Munich falls victim to a devastating fire (also in 1418, 1432 and 1590).
1328	Ludwig IV 'the Bavarian' is made Holy Roman Emperor and Munich becomes temporarily the imperial capital.
1505	Munich becomes the capital of Bavaria.
1618–48	Gustav Adolph of Sweden occupies Munich in the Thirty Years' War.
1634	The plague reduces Munich's population by one third to 9,000.
1806	Bavaria becomes a kingdom.
1810	A horse race to celebrate the marriage of Crown Prince Ludwig starts the tradition of the Oktoberfest.
1825–48	King Ludwig I tranforms Munich into the 'Athens on the Isar', a flourishing centre of art and learning, and a university city.
1848	Ludwig I abdicates following political unrest and an affair with dancer Lola Montez.
1864	Richard Wagner moves here under the patronage of 'fairy-tale' King Ludwig II.
1876	First trams (horse drawn) run in Munich.
1886	Ludwig II is certified insane and later found mysteriously drowned in Lake Starnberg.
1900	Munich becomes a centre of the Jugendstil (Art Nouveau) movement.

1918	King Ludwig III is deposed in the Bavarian Revolution, led by Kurt Eisner, Bavaria's first Prime Minister.
1919	Eisner's assassination in Munich leads to the establishment of a soviet-style republic and its bloody defeat in May.
1923	Hitler's *putsch* fails.
1933	Hitler comes to power.
1939	Outbreak of World War II.
1940	First air attack on Munich (there are another 70 before 1945).
1945	Munich is taken by American troops. With half its buildings destroyed, a huge rebuilding plan begins.
1946	Munich becomes the capital of the Free State of Bavaria.
1965–72	Construction of the U- and S-Bahn network.
1972	The 20th Summer Olympic Games, held in Munich, ends in tragedy following a terrorist attack.
1980	A bomb attack during the Oktoberfest claims 12 lives.
1990	Reunification of Germany enables many emigrants from eastern Europe and the former GDR to settle in Munich.
1992	World Economic Summit Meeting is held in Munich. The new airport is opened. Over 400,000 people participate in Germany's first *Lichterkette* (candle vigils) in Munich, protesting against violence against foreigners and minorities.
1995	City councils start discussions ('Perspektive München') on city development.

11

PEOPLE & EVENTS FROM HISTORY

Cartoon of Richard Strauss, one of the world's most popular composers

Thomas Mann's shining city

'München leuchtete' ('Munich shone'), the opening words of *Gladius Dei* (1902) by Thomas Mann, is without doubt one of Munich's most famous quotations. Mann, a resident of Munich, became one of Germany's most celebrated writers, receiving the Nobel Prize for Literature in 1929. Today, Munich remains Mann's shining city, his words stamped on its medal of honour 'Munich shines – on Munich's friends'.

RICHARD STRAUSS

Richard Strauss was born in Munich in 1864, and eventually became Kapellmeister (musical director) of the city. The breathtaking Bavarian scenery held a magnetic attraction for him, influencing his compositions considerably, and was particularly evident in his *'Alpensinfonie'*. His operas still rate among the most popular throughout the world and a striking fountain, depicting dramatic scenes from *Salome*, stands in the city centre as a fitting memorial to Munich's greatest composer.

LUDWIG II

Although King Ludwig II's extravagant 'fairy-tale' castles were a drain on the regency's treasury, today they are the most popular and profitable tourist attractions in Bavaria (► 20). Since childhood, Ludwig had a passion for German legend as epitomised in the operas of Richard Wagner. Following a performance of *Lohengrin*, Ludwig became an enthusiastic admirer and patron of Wagner, whose works provided inspiration for his eccentric building plans. As state affairs became increasingly neglected, the doomed monarch was declared insane and, shortly after, met a mysterious watery death on the eastern shore of Lake Starnberg.

ADOLF HITLER & THE BEER HALL PUTSCH

Hitler once said 'Munich is the city closest to my heart. Here as a young man, as a soldier and as a politician I made my start'. He made his first bid for power here in the famous Beer Hall Putsch of 1923, launching his career as leader of the Nazi party. It began when he stormed a meeting of local dignitaries in the Bürgerbräukeller and ended in bloodshed at Odeonsplatz, after which he was sent to prison. Here he wrote *Mein Kampf* ('My Struggle'). Undeterred, following his release nine months later, Hitler inspired his movement, which continued to gain momentum, enabling him to seize power in 1933.

MUNICH
how to organise your time

ITINERARIES

These four suggested itineraries will help you cover some of Munich's main sights, aided by the excellent transport system. Use the efficient underground (U-Bahn) and suburban trains (S-Bahn) or, for a more scenic ride, the buses and trams. The city centre, however, is best explored on foot.

ITINERARY ONE	**THE CITY CENTRE**
Morning	Take the U- or S-Bahn to Karlsplatz (Stachus) and spend the morning shopping in Munich's pedestrianised city centre Pause for a coffee in Café Glockenspiel (➤ 64) in Marienplatz around 11 to watch the famous Glockenspiel in action (➤ 37) Don't miss the Viktualienmarkt (➤ 40) and the smart boutiques of Theatinerstrasse, Residenzstrasse and Maximilianstrasse (➤ 70)
Lunch	Choose one of Marienplatz's many cafés and *Keller*, perhaps the Ratskeller under the New Town Hall (➤ 63), for lunch
Afternoon	Head southwards to the City Museum (➤ 35) to discover Munich's history If you still have presents and souvenirs to buy, you should find something in Sendlingerstrasse, but allow time to visit the magnificent Asamkirche (➤ 34)
ITINERARY TWO	**ART & ANTIQUITIES**
Morning	Travel by U-Bahn to Königsplatz where a choice of three museums and galleries awaits you: the Sculpture Museum (Glyptothek ➤ 30), the State Collection of Antiquities (Staatliche Antikensammlung ➤ 30) and the City Gallery in the Lenbachhaus (➤ 29)
Lunch	Walk northwards along Barerstrasse for a light lunch in the Brasserie Trzesniewski (➤ 65), opposite the Neue Pinakothek
Afternoon	Spend a relaxing afternoon exploring the classical and modern collections of the Alte and Neue Pinakothek galleries (➤ 31, 32)

ITINERARY THREE	**PARKS & PALACES**
Morning	Take the U-Bahn to Rotkreuzplatz, then tram 12 to visit Schloss Nymphenburg (➤ 24) Spend some time in the gardens and pause for coffee in the Palmhouse Café
Lunch	Have lunch at Zur Schwaige in the south wing of the palace (➤ 63), then return on foot along the Nymphenburg canal and back down Nymphenburger Strasse to Rotkreuzplatz. Alternatively, shop in the food hall of Dallmayr, Munich's finest delicatessen, near Marienplatz (➤ 72) and have a picnic in the pleasant grounds of the Hofgarten (➤ 41)
Afternoon	Visit the opulent royal Residenz with its 112 rooms crammed full of priceless treasures, and the Cuvilliés Theatre (➤ 42)
ITINERARY FOUR	**ANCIENT & MODERN MUNICH**
Morning	Travel to Isartor S-Bahn station. Walk along Zweibrückenstrasse towards the river and the Deutsches Museum (➤ 45)
Lunch	Enjoy a light lunch in the museum restaurant overlooking the River Isar, or take a snack in an old converted railroad carriage
Afternoon	You could easily spend all day at the Deutsches Museum Alternatively, wander along the east bank of the Isar, past the Maximilaneum, home of the Bavarian parliament, and the Angel of Peace statue (Friedensengel ➤ 58), then westwards along Prinzregentenstrasse to admire the treasures of the Bavarian National Museum (➤ 48) Late afternoon is always a particularly pleasant time to stroll through the English Garden to the Seehaus beer garden (➤ 47)

WALKS

Coat of arms on the Archbishop's Palace

INFORMATION

Distance 3km
Time 2 hours
Start point Odeonsplatz
⊞ N24
▣ U-Bahn Odeonsplatz
End point Max-Joseph-Platz
⊞ N24
▣ U-Bahn Odeonsplatz

MUNICH'S OLD TOWN

From Odeonsplatz walk down Brienner-strasse with its expensive antique shops. After a short distance the elegant Wittelsbacherplatz opens out to the right, with an impressive equestrian statue of Elector Maximilian I. Soon afterwards, turn left at Amiraplatz, past the Greek Orthodox Salvatorkirche, and on into Kardinal-Faulhaber-Strasse where the distinctive domes of Frauenkirche tower over its spectacular façades. The Archbishop's Palace at No. 48 has been the residence of the archbishops of Munich and Freising since 1818. Turn into Promenadeplatz, past one of Munich's best hotels, the Bayerische Hof, the Carmelite Church (the earliest baroque church in Munich) on your left and the Church of the Holy Trinity opposite. Pass by Munich's Wittelsbach fountain (1885) at the main road, before turning left towards Mövenpick, one of the city's finest coffee houses.

After coffee, continue along the main road until Karlsplatz (Stachus). Pass through Karlstor (site of the former west gate to the city) into the pedestrian zone (Neuhauser Strasse). Don't miss Michaelskirche, designed as a monument to the Counter-Reformation, before turning left along Augustinerstrasse to Munich's cathedral, the Frauenkirche. Return to the main shopping precinct via Liebfrauenstrasse and continue on to Marienplatz.

If you're feeling energetic, the view of the city centre from the Peterskirche tower is worth the effort. Swing round the side of the church to the Viktualienmarkt. Return to Marienplatz and walk up Dienerstrasse to enjoy a traditional Bavarian lunch in Spatenhaus (➤ 63) on Max-Joseph-Platz.

GARDENS & GALLERIES

Walk past the grand Residenz, home to the great Wittelsbach rulers and art collectors for five centuries, towards Odeonsplatz, then head eastwards into the enchanting Hofgarten (Court Garden), beautifully laid out with neat flowerbeds and fountains. Cut diagonally across the gardens, past the Staatskanzlei (State Chancellery) building, finished in 1994, and continue down a narrow path alongside the Finance Garden. Cross Von-der-Tann-Strasse by the pedestrian subway to the Haus der Kunst, Munich's impressive modern art gallery, housed in a monumental building of the Third Reich.

The famous English Garden is just a stone's throw from the gallery. Head towards the Monopteros or Lovers' Temple, one of the park's great landmarks, for splendid views of Munich's skyline. Stop at the Chinese Tower, site of Munich's most popular beer garden, for light refreshment, then leave the English Garden to the west via Veterinärstrasse until you reach the University, marked by two magnificent bowl fountains. Turn left into Ludwigstrasse, a grand avenue laid out by Ludwig I to display the wealth of his flourishing kingdom. The Ludwigskirche (Ludwig's Church) on your left contains one of the world's largest frescoes.

Cross over Ludwigstrasse opposite the church into Schellingstrasse, just one of the maze of streets behind the university, bursting with student life in its numerous bars and cafés, design shops and bookshops. A left turn into Barerstrasse leads to Munich's two other great galleries; the New Picture Gallery (Neue Pinakothek) with its extensive 19th- and early 20th-century collections, followed by the Old Picture Gallery (Alte Pinakothek), one of the world's greatest galleries of Old Master paintings.

The Chinese Tower in the English Garden

THE SIGHTS

- Residenz (➤ 42)
- Odeonsplatz (➤ 41)
- Hofgarten (➤ 41)
- House of Art (➤ 46)
- English Garden (➤ 47)
- Ludwigskirche (➤ 57)
- New Picture Gallery (➤ 32)
- Old Picture Gallery (➤ 31)

INFORMATION

Distance 4km
Time 2 hours
Start point Max-Joseph-Platz
　N24
　U-Bahn Odeonsplatz
End point Old Picture Gallery
　M23
　Tram 27

EVENING STROLLS

Window shopping in Marienplatz

SCHWABING

Schwabing, mecca of Munich's fashion scene by day, becomes a riot of cafés and restaurants frequented by a trendy international crowd by night. To check out some of the best nightspots, start at Münchener Freiheit and walk southwards along Leopoldstrasse. This is the place to see and be seen, with an almost Italian atmosphere of ice-cream parlours and cafés spilling out on to broad pavement terraces. Turn right before Ludwig I's Victory Arch into Akademiestrasse then left into Amalienstrasse, where the streets buzz with life. Continue briefly along Theresienstrasse before turning up Türkenstrasse, one of Schwabing's most lively streets, as far as Georgenstrasse. The cosy Georgenhof restaurant at the junction, with its open fires and wholesome cooking, is a perfect way to complete the evening.

ROYAL MUNICH

Just behind Marienplatz lies a maze of narrow little lanes which have retained their medieval character. Immediately in front of the Old Town Hall, go down Burgstrasse, the oldest street in the city, past the homes of former residents, Mozart and Cuvilliés. Continue through the archway of the old royal residence (Alter Hof), then right past the Central Mint (Münzhof) along Pfisterstrasse to the royal brewery, Hofbräuhaus (►43). Turn left up to the bright lights and dazzling designer windows of the exclusive Maximilianstrasse, then left towards the magnificently illuminated Nationaltheater (►44). Head back along Dienerstrasse, past the former royal delicatessen, Dallmayr, to Marienplatz. If you resisted a drink at the Hofbräuhaus, the tiny Jodlerwirt rates as one of the most atmospheric, typically Bavarian watering-holes.

ORGANISED SIGHTSEEING

ON FOOT & BY BUS

MUNICH TOURIST OFFICE
A wide range of tours provide a thorough survey of the Bavarian metropolis. Also personal tailor-made tours (minimum 2 hours).
✉ Sendlingerstrasse 1 ☎ 2 33 30–234

MÜNCHENER STADT-RUNDFAHRTEN
Special tours include *Munich by Night* and city tours combined with the Bavaria Film Studios or the Olympiapark.
✉ Arnulfstrasse 8 ☎ 12 04 418

STATTREISEN MÜNCHEN
A variety of specialist walking tours including 'National Socialism and Resistance' (Munich's development as a Nazi 'capital'), 'Hops and Malt' (why Munich promotes itself as the 'Beer City'), 'Salt & Chips' (looking at Munich's industry) and 'Schwabing', exploring the city's intellectual, artistic heart.
☎ 271 89 40

BY BIKE

CITYHOPPER TOUREN
Choose between two cycle tours: the 2-hour *Old Town Tour* or the 4-hour *Romantic Tour* through Munich's main parks.
✉ Hohenzollernstrasse 95 ☎ 272 11 31

SPURWECHSEL
Bike tours with political or historical themes; also a NaTour 'green' tour.
☎ 69 24 699

BY TRAM

STATTREISEN MÜNCHEN
Explore Munich by tram.
☎ 271 89 40

The Hofbräuhaus, Munich's best-known beer hall

Out-of-town excursions
A number of tour operators offer excursions to nearby tourist attractions including day-trips to Neuschwanstein (➤ 20), Zugspitze (Germany's highest mountain), Berchtesgaden and Salzburg. Contact Bavarian Travel Bureau (☎ 12 04–0), Panorama Tours (☎ 12 04–418) or Autobus Oberbayern (☎ 5 52 56 40).

EXCURSIONS

Neuschwanstein Castle

INFORMATION

Neuschwanstein

Distance 120km

Journey time About 2 hours

📷 Guided tours 9–5:30
(summer), 10–4 (winter)

🚌 Daily bus excursions with
Panorama Tours (➤ 19)

➕ Off map to southwest

Tourist Information

✉ Münchenerstrasse 2,
Schwangau

☎ (08362) 81051

Augsburg

Distance 60km

Journey time 30 minutes

🚆 Frequent trains from the
main station

➕ Off map to northwest

✉ Bahnhofstrasse 7

☎ (0821) 502070

NEUSCHWANSTEIN

The fairy-tale Disneyland castle really does exist, a magical white-turreted affair nestled in a pine forest in the foothills of the Bavarian Alps. In an attempt to make the fantasy world of Wagnerian opera a reality, 'Mad' King Ludwig commissioned a stage designer rather than an architect to design this romantic, theatrical castle, and watched it being built by telescope from his father's neighbouring castle of Hohenschwangau. Sadly only 15 of the 65 rooms were finished and he had only spent a few days there before he was dethroned (➤ 12). Nevertheless, the lavish interior is worth queuing up for, with its extravagant décor and vast wall paintings of Wagnerian scenes. Fortunately Ludwig's request to destroy the castle on his death was ignored and today it is Bavaria's number-one tourist attraction.

AUGSBURG

Augsburg, one of Germany's oldest cities, was founded in 15BC as *Augusta Vindelicorum* but had its heyday during the Renaissance as one of Europe's richest cultural centres. Today, this lively university town, Bavaria's third-largest city, offers a fine array of impressive Renaissance buildings, including the palace and chapel of the wealthy Fugger family and the Fuggerei, eight streets of gabled houses built in 1519 to house the town's poor, which still takes in citizens in need. Other Augsburg celebrities include Martin Luther (the city played a vital role in the Reformation with its unique 'double' churches), Mozart's father and Bertolt Brecht (both born here), and Rudolf Diesel, who invented the fuel engine here in 1897.

BAD TÖLZ

The beautiful spa town of Bad Tölz is famous for its health cures, based on its iodine-rich springs and peat baths. The traffic-free cobbled main street – Marktstrasse – lined with handsome pastel-coloured houses ornately decorated with murals, leads up to the twin-spired Kreuzkirche with its Leonhard chapel. Every year on St Leonhard's Day (6 November), locals bring their horses to be blessed here by the patron saint of animals in an entertaining festival called the Leonhard Ride.

Located at the foot of the Bavarian Alps, Bad Tölz makes a perfect base for mountain walks, skiing and sporting activities. Children enjoy the nearby Blombergbahn – Germany's longest summer toboggan run and scene in winter of a crazy sled-flying competition, which attracts thousands of spectators.

CHIEMSEE

Locally called the 'Bavarian Sea', Chiemsee is the largest of the Bavarian lakes. Its lush scenery and picture-postcard Alpine backdrop has attracted artists for centuries and today draws holidaymakers from all over Germany to its shores for swimming, sailing and other pursuits.

Take a boat trip from Prien, the largest and loveliest town on the lake, and explore the Herreninsel and Fraueninsel (Men's Island and Women's Island), whose names originate from the 8th-century Benedictine monastery and nunnery there. The lake's main attraction, however, is Herrenchiemsee, site of Ludwig II's most ambitious palace – a replica of the Château of Versailles. Only the central wing of the building was completed, including the spectacular Hall of Mirrors.

INFORMATION

Bad Tölz
Distance 40km
Journey time 1 hour

- 🚉 Hourly trains from the main station
- ➕ Off map to south

Tourist Information

- ✉ Ludwigstrasse 11
- ☎ (08041) 70071

Chiemsee
Distance 80km
Journey time 1 hour

- 🕐 Guided palace tours 9–5 (summer), 10–4 (winter)
- 🚉 Frequent trains to Prien from the main station
- ➕ Off map to southeast

Tourist Information

- ✉ Alte Rathausstrasse 11, Prien am Chiemsee
- ☎ (08051) 2280 and (08051) 6090 (for ferry information)

Schloss Herrenchiemsee

WHAT'S ON

Over 100 days a year are officially devoted to processions, parties and festivals. You can find details in the Tourist Office's *Official Monthly Calendar of Events* or the monthly English-language magazine *Munich Found*.

FEBRUARY	*Fasching* (➤ 52)
MARCH	*Strong Beer Season* (➤ 52)
APRIL	*Spring Festival* (mid-April for two weeks): a mini-Oktoberfest at the Theresienwiese
	Ballet Festival Week (end May)
	Auer Mai Dult (end April/early May): the first of three annual fairs and flea markets
MAY	*May Day* (1 May): traditional dancing round the maypole at the Viktualienmarkt
	Maibockzeit: a season of special strong lagers, originating from North Germany
	Corpus Christi (second Thursday after Whitsun): this magnificent Catholic procession has been taking place ever since 1343
	Spargelzeit ('Asparagus Time'): it's surprising how many ways there are to serve asparagus
JUNE	*Founding of Munich* (14 June): from Marienplatz to Odeonsplatz the streets come alive with music, street theatre and refreshment stalls
	Film Festival (last week in June): a week of international cinematic art
	Tollwood Festival (end June): the Olympiapark hosts an 'alternative' festival of rock, jazz, cabaret, food and folklore
JULY	*Jacobi Dult* (mid-July): the second annual *Dult*
	Opera Festival (mid-July): the climax of Munich's cultural year
	Kocherlball (mid-July): a traditional 'workers' ball at 6AM in the English Garden
AUGUST	*Summer Festival* (mid-August): a fortnight of fireworks, festivities and frolicking in the Olympiapark
SEPTEMBER	*Oktoberfest* (➤ 52)
OCTOBER	*Kirchweih Dult* (end October): the third annual *Dult*
	German Art and Antiques Fair (end October)
DECEMBER	*Christkindlmarkt* (➤ 52)
	Compaq Grand Slam Cup (early December): one of the most prestigious and glamorous events in international tennis

MUNICH's
top 25 sights

The sights are shown on the maps on the inside front cover and inside back cover, numbered **1–25** *from west to east across the city*

1

SCHLOSS NYMPHENBURG

Exhibit in the Marstallmuseum

INFORMATION

- L18–19
- 17 90 80
- Oct–Mar, Tue–Sun 10–12:30, 1:30–4; Apr–Sep, 9–12:30, 1:30–5. Closed Mon and bank holidays
  Gardens: daily 7–dusk
  Botanical Gardens: Oct–Mar, daily 9–4:30; Apr–Sep, 9–6
- Café Palmenhaus (££)
- U-Bahn Rotkreuzplatz
- Tram 17; bus 41
- None
- Moderate
- Museum of Mankind and Nature (Museum Mensch und Natur) (➤ 60)

"Hard to believe that one of Germany's largest baroque palaces, set in magnificent parkland, started life as a modest summer villa. This arcadian corner of Munich is one of the city's loveliest recreation areas."

The palace Five generations of Bavarian royalty were involved in the construction of this vast, gleaming palace, starting with Elector Ferdinand Maria. Thrilled by the birth of his heir Max Emanuel, he had the central section built in the style of an Italian villa by Agostino Barelli (1664–74) for his wife. Each succeeding ruler added another wing or pavilion, resulting in a majestic, semicircular construction, stretching 500m from one wing to the other.

The interior The central structure contains sumptuous galleries, including the majestic rococo Stone Hall and Ludwig I's 'Gallery of Beauties', featuring 36 Munich ladies, some said to have been the king's mistresses. In the old stables, the Marstallmuseum's dazzling collection of state carriages and sleighs recalls the heyday of the Wittelsbach family and the Porcelain Museum provides a comprehensive history of the famous Nymphenburg porcelain factory since its foundation in 1761.

Park and pavilions Originally in Italian then French baroque style, in 1803 Ludwig von Sckell transformed the gardens into a fashionable English park with ornate waterways, statues, pavilions and a maze. See yourself reflected 10-fold in the Hall of Mirrors in the Amalienburg hunting lodge; visit the Magdalenenklause, an unusual shell-encrusted hermitage; or the Badenburg, said to be Europe's first post-Roman heated pool.

OLYMPIAPARK

❝Since the 1972 Olympics the park, with its intriguing skyline, has become one of the city's landmarks and a favourite place for leisure and relaxation. Its tower offers an unforgettable view of Munich and the Alps.❞

The Olympic Site In 1972, the historic Oberwiesenfeld, a former royal Bavarian parade ground to the north of the city centre, was chosen for the 20th Summer Olympics. In 1909 the first airship landed here and from 1925 until 1939 it was the site of Munich's airport. Used as a dump during World War II, it was eventually transformed in 1968 into a multi-functional sport and recreation area.

The buildings The television tower, built between 1965 and 1968, the tallest reinforced concrete construction in Europe, was renamed Olympiaturm in honour of the Games. Visit the viewing platform and revolving restaurant on a clear day for a breathtaking Alpine panorama and a magical view of the city at night. Together with the futuristic tent-roof, it has become a symbol of modern Munich. This netlike roof construction resembles an immense spider's web and cost DM168 million, making it the most expensive roof in the world. Tour the area on the little train to see the Olympiasee, an artificial lake; the Olympiaberg, a 53m hill constructed from wartime rubble; the quaint Russian Orthodox chapel built by Father Timothy, a Russian recluse, decorated inside with thousands of pieces of silver paper; and the Olympic Village, sadly remembered today as the scene of the terrorist attack on 11 Israeli athletes on 5 September 1972.

DID YOU KNOW?

- The Olympic park covers more than 3sq km
- The Olympiaturm is 290m high
- The Olympic Stadium (home to FC Bayern soccer club) (➤ 83) holds 70,000 people
- The Olympic village houses around 9,000 people

INFORMATION

- ✚ J/K22
- ✉ Spiridon-Louis-Ring 21
- ☎ 30 67 2414/2416
- 🕐 Olympiaturm: 9–midnight Olympiastadion: Nov–Mar 9–4:30; Apr–Oct 8:30–6
- 🍴 Revolving restaurant (££)
- Ⓤ U-Bahn Olympiazentrum
- 🚌 Tram 20, 21, 27; bus 36, 41, 43, 81, 136, 184
- ↔ BMW Museum (➤ 26)

The Olympiaturm

3

BMW-MUSEUM

INFORMATION

- J22
- Petuelring 130
- 38 22 56 52
- Daily 9–5
- U-Bahn Olympiazentrum, Petuelring
- Tram 27; Bus 36, 41, 43, 81, 136
- Excellent
- Moderate
- Olympiapark (➤ 25)
- The museum has a special guide in English for children aged eight and upwards. Phone in advance for a factory tour

"Even if the high-tech world of automobiles doesn't particularly interest you, you cannot fail to marvel at the developments of transport technology over the past five generations presented at this, the most popular company museum in Germany."

The museum The BMW 'Time Horizon' Museum, housed in a gleaming, silver, windowless half sphere, provides an eye-catching contrast to the adjacent high-rise headquarters of the Bavarian Motor Works (➤ 59) and its surrounding factory buildings. With over a quarter of a million visitors annually, the reason for its success is not only its fascinating display of very rare cars and motorcycles, but the excellent view it gives of the past through non-stop videos and slide shows (all with English commentary), covering such subjects as changing family life and work conditions, the role of women in industry, and car recycling (in which BMW is at the forefront of development). There are even excerpts of old science fiction films including *Frankenstein*, *2001* and George Orwell's *1984*.

Future vision Take a journey into the future with electric or solar-generated hydrogen-drive cars or design your own model and watch it develop step-by-step on computer. Adults and children vie with each other to sit in the cockpit of tomorrow's car and experiment with its highly sophisticated data and information systems. At the museum's cinema, 'Emotions in Motion' is a reminder of how all this new technology improves our world by giving us more time to enjoy and respect nature and the environment. Your visit is neatly summed up by the company's motto, 'Sheer Driving Pleasure'.

DACHAU

"Once people visited Dachau to see the Renaissance château and town, until it became synonymous with the Nazi reign of terror. Today the concentration camp (KZ Gedenkstätte) has been preserved as a memorial to those who died here.**"**

Summer castle The pretty little town of Dachau, with its 18th-century pastel facades and quaint cobbled streets, is set on the steep bank of the Amper River. Above the town, the Renaissance castle was once a popular summer residence of the Munich Royals. Only one wing of the original four survives, but it contains a large banqueting hall with one of the most exquisitely carved ceilings in Bavaria. Near by, the Dachauer Moos, a heathy area often wreathed in mists, has a delicate light much loved by artists.

Münchners used to come to Dachau to wander its picturesque cobbled streets and visit the castle. But on 22nd March 1933, only 50 days after Hitler came to power, Dachau was designated as the site of the first concentration camp of the Third Reich.

The Concentration Camp Although it was not one of the main extermination camps, 31,951 deaths were recorded here between 1933 and 1945. Several of the original buildings have been restored as a memorial, a poignant reminder of the fate suffered by the 206,000 inmates. The museum documents the camp's history in an attempt to show objectively the atrocities that happened here. The gates still bear the bitterly ironic slogan 'Arbeit macht frei' ('Work makes you free').

INFORMATION

- ✚ Off map to northwest
- Ⓢ S-Bahn Dachau

The Concentration Camp
- ✉ Alte Römerstrasse 75
- ☎ (081 31) 17 41
- ◷ Tue–Sun 9–5
- 🚌 bus 722 to Robert-Bosch-Strasse
- ♿ Excellent
- 💷 Free
- ❓ Documentary film in English at 11:30 and 3:30

Memorial to the dead

DEN TOTEN
ZUR EHR
DEN LEBENDEN
ZUR MAHNUNG

5

SCHLEISSHEIM PALACES

HIGHLIGHTS

Old Palace
● Gallery of religious folk art
New Palace
● Great Gallery
Palace Lustheim
● Meissen Porcelain Museum

INFORMATION

✚ Off map to north

☎ 315 52 72 (Old Palace); 315 87 20 (New and Lustheim)

🕐 Old Palace: Tue–Sun 10–5; New Palace, Lustheim Palace, Porcelain Museum: Tue–Sun 10–12:30, 1:30–5 (until 4 Oct–Mar)

🚊 S-Bahn Oberschleissheim

🚌 Bus 292

♿ None

💷 Cheap

Meissen chinoiserie, Schloss Lustheim

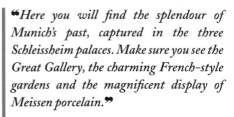

❝*Here you will find the splendour of Munich's past, captured in the three Schleissheim palaces. Make sure you see the Great Gallery, the charming French-style gardens and the magnificent display of Meissen porcelain.***❞**

Old Palace In 1597 Duke Wilhelm V bought a farm to the east of the Dachau moor as a retirement residence. His son, Prince Elector Maximilian I, later transformed it into an Italian-style Renaissance palace. He called it the Altes Schloss Schleissheim. Today it contains part of the Bavarian National Museum, including an unusual gallery devoted to international religious folk art.

New Palace (Neues Schloss) The beautiful 'Versailles of Munich' was commissioned by Prince Elector Max Emanuel II as a summer residence. It was the largest palace complex of its day, demonstrating his wealth and power. Despite severe damage during World War II, the sumptuous rococo interior remained largely intact. The Great Gallery, over 60m long, contains the Bavarian State Art Collection. Acknowledged as one of the most remarkable collections of baroque paintings in Europe, it has around a thousand paintings, including masterpieces by Rubens, Titian, Veronese and van Dyck.

Palace Lustheim Separated from the New Palace by delightful formal gardens and a decorative canal which encircles it, Palace Lustheim (Schloss Lustheim), originally accessible only by boat, was planned as an island of happiness for Max Emanuel's bride Maria Antonia. It houses Germany's largest collection of Meissen porcelain.

LENBACHHAUS: CITY GALLERY

❝ *This beautiful gallery displays predominantly 19th- and 20th-century works of art. The tiny formal garden is also a delight – a harmonious blend of modern and classical statuary and fountains.* **❞**

The Lenbachhaus This charming villa was built in 1887 in Florentine High Renaissance style by Gabriel von Seidl for the 'painter prince' Franz von Lenbach, darling of the German aristocracy and the most fashionable Bavarian painter of his day. After his death, it became the property of the city and was converted into the municipal art gallery (Städtische Galerie im Lenbachhaus). A north wing was added in the late 1920s to balance the south wing, where Lenbach's studio was housed. The resulting structure perfectly frames the terrace and ornamental gardens.

The collections The chief objective of the City Gallery is to document the development of painting in Munich from the late Gothic period up to the present day. Munich 'Romantics' and landscape artists, including Spitzweg, Leibl, Defregger, Lenbach and Corinth are well represented, as is the *Jugendstil* period. However, it is the paintings by the Munich-based expressionist *Der Blaue Reiter* (Blue Rider) group which gained the Lenbachhaus international fame, including over 300 works by Wassily Kandinsky, who founded the movement with Franz Marc. Paul Klee, Gabriele Münter, August Macke and Alexej von Jawlensky are well represented, along with a collection of dazzling contemporary art by Anselm Kiefer, Andy Warhol, Roy Lichtenstein, Josef Beuys and others.

HIGHLIGHTS

- Kandinsky collection
- *Der Blaue Reiter* collection
- *Show your Wounds*, Joseph Beuys
- *Blue Horse*, Franz Marc
- Munich *Jugendstil* collection

The formal Italian garden.
Top: Jawlensky und Werefkin *by Münter*

INFORMATION

- ✚ M23
- ✉ Luisenstrasse 33
- ☎ Tue–Sun 10–6
- 🍴 Café and garden terrace (££)
- Ⓤ U-Bahn Königsplatz
- ♿ Good
- 💶 Expensive
- ↔ Königsplatz (➤ 30), Old Picture Gallery (➤ 31), New Picture Gallery (➤ 32)
- ❓ *Der Blaue Reiter* guided tours are organised by the Munich Volkshochschule, Wed at 10, Sun at 11

7

KÖNIGSPLATZ

HIGHLIGHTS

Glyptothek
- Barberinian Faun (*above*)
- Mnesarete tomb relief
- Aeginetan marbles
- Crowned bust of Emperor Augustus
- Mosaic pavement from Sentinum
- Boy with a goose

Staatliche Antikensammlung
- Exekesias and Dionysus kraters
- Helikon-Lekythos
- Funeral wreath of Armento
- Athenian theatre masks

INFORMATION

- ✚ M23
- ✉ Königsplatz
- ☎ Glyptothek 286100; Antikensammlung 598359
- 🕐 Glyptothek: Tue, Wed, Fri–Sun 10–4:30; Thu noon–8:30
  Antikensammlung: Tue, Thu–Sun 10–4:30; Wed noon–8:30
- 🍴 Glyptothek museum café (£)
- Ⓤ U-Bahn Königsplatz
- ♿ Good (Glyptothek); none (Antikensammlung)
- 💷 Moderate
- ↔ Municipal Art Gallery in the Lenbachhaus (➤ 29), Old Picture Gallery (➤ 31), New Picture Gallery (➤ 32)
- ❓ Free guided tour at 6PM on Wednesday at the Antikensammlung

" *This spacious, majestic square, nick-named 'Athens-on-the-Isar', and flanked by three immense neo-classical temples, may come as a surprise in the heart of Munich. However, you needn't be a scholar to enjoy a stroll here.* **"**

The Square and the Propyläen Along with the buildings of Ludwigstrasse, Königsplatz represents Ludwig I's greatest contribution to Munich. Laid out by Leo von Klenze, according to plans by Carl von Fischer, the square took 50 years to complete, from 1812 to 1862. The final building, the Propyläen, modelled on the entrance to the Athenian Acropolis, is the most striking.

Nazi control Between 1933 and 1935, the appearance of Königsplatz was completely transformed. Hitler paved over the grass-covered, tree-lined square and Königsplatz became the National Socialists' 'Akropolis Germaniae' – an impressive setting for Nazi rallies. Recently, the paving stones were replaced by broad expanses of lawn, enabling Königsplatz to return to its former serenity.

Museums The Glyptothek or Sculpture Museum on the north flank of Königsplatz is not only the oldest museum in Munich but also one of the most celebrated neo-classical buildings in Germany. The interior houses one of the foremost collections of ancient Greek and Roman sculpture in Europe. To the south, the Corinithian-style Staatliche Antikensammlung (State Collection of Antiquities) contains a priceless collection of ancient vases, jewellery, bronzes and terra-cotta sculptures.

ALTE PINAKOTHEK

"A treasure house for experts and amateurs alike – over 850 Old Master paintings in a massive museum, rated alongside the Louvre, Uffizi, Prado and Metropolitan as one of the world's most important galleries."

Architectural masterpiece The Old Picture Gallery represents the pinnacle of Bavaria's centuries-old dedication to the arts. It was commissioned by Ludwig I and designed by Leo von Klenze to replace the older Kammergalerie in the Residenz, which had become too small for the Royal Collection. The gallery, modelled on the Renaissance palaces of Venice, took ten years to build and on completion in 1836 was proclaimed a masterpiece – the largest gallery building of its time and a model for other museum buildings in Rome and Brussels. During World War II it was so badly damaged that demolition was contemplated. However, it was restored in the '50s. At the end of a four-year face-lift in the '90s the magnificent gallery will provide a fitting backdrop for one of the world's finest collections of Western paintings. (Until then, the most important works can be seen in the Neue Pinakothek.)

Priceless treasures All the main schools of European art from the Middle Ages to the beginning of the 19th century are represented in this museum, with the emphasis on German, Dutch and Flemish paintings, including works by Dürer, van Dyck, Breughel and over 100 by Rubens (the finest collection of its kind in the world).

HIGHLIGHTS

- *Fool's Paradise,* Pieter Breughel the Elder
- *Four Apostles,* Dürer
- *Adoration of the Magi,* Tiepolo
- *Madonna Tempi,* Raphael
- *The Great Last Judgement,* Rubens
- *The Resurrection,* Rembrandt

INFORMATION

- ✚ M23
- ✉ Barerstrasse 27
- ☎ 23 80 52 16
- ◷ Tue–Sun 9:15–4:30; also Tue and Thu 7–9PM
- Ⓢ U-Bahn Königsplatz
- 🚃 Tram 27
- ♿ Very good
- 💷 Moderate
- ⬌ New Picture Galley (➤ 32)

Dürer's Four Apostles

NEUE PINAKOTHEK

HIGHLIGHTS

- *Ostende*, William Turner
- *Breakfast*, Edouard Manet
- *Vase with Sunflowers* and *View of Arles*, Vincent van Gogh
- *Large Reclining Woman*, Henry Moore

The Laundress, *Degas*

INFORMATION

- ➕ M23
- ➕ Barerstrasse 29
- ☎ 23 80 51 95
- ⏰ Tue–Sun 10–5; Tue and Thu until 8
- 🍴 Café with terrace (££)
- Ⓤ U-Bahn Theresienstrasse
- 🚃 Tram 27
- ♿ Very good
- 💷 Moderate
- ↔ Old Picture Gallery (➤ 31)

32

"*The New Picture Gallery, the largest post-war gallery in Germany, is a shining modern contrast to the Renaissance style of the Old Picture Gallery across the road, and carries the collections on through the 19th and early 20th centuries of art.* **"**

'Palazzo Branca' As with the Old Picture Gallery (Alte Pinakothek), it was Ludwig I who instigated the building of this gallery for contemporary arts in 1846. However, following extensive damage in World War II, a competition was held in 1966 to design a new gallery in the heart of Schwabing, Munich's trendy student quarter.

The winning entry was designed by Munich architect Alexander von Branca. It was built at a staggering cost of DM105 million and opened in 1981 – an attractive concrete, granite and glass structure (sometimes named 'Palazzo Branca') which integrates art deco and post-modernist designs with traditional features in an unusual figure-of-eight formation around two inner courtyards and terraced ponds.

Art treasures The gallery boasts over 600 paintings, drawings and sculptures spanning a variety of periods from rococo to art nouveau (*Jugendstil*), focusing on the development of German art alongside English 19th-century landscapes and portraits, and French Impressionism. It is best to follow the rooms in chronological order, starting with early Romantic works, then on through French and German late Romanticism, French and German Impressionism and finally Symbolist and art nouveau works.

MICHAELSKIRCHE

"You would be forgiven for not immediately spotting the Michaelskirche, but behind its striking façade lies the largest Renaissance church north of the Alps – a sight not to be missed."

Eventful construction The Jesuit Church of St Michael was built at the end of the 16th century by Duke Wilhelm (the Pious) as a monument to the Counter-Reformation. Disaster struck in 1590 when the tower collapsed, but it was finally consecrated in 1597. Severe wartime damage has been masterfully repaired and you will marvel at the vast Renaissance hall with its ornate, barrel-vaulted roof.

The façade The bold late-Renaissance façade is unified by its consistency of round-headed windows, doorways and niches. In the true combative spirit of the Counter-Reformation, it is fitting that these niches contain stone figures of the Wittelsbach dukes and emperors – secular defenders of the faith – including a splendid figure of the church's patron, Wilhelm V. The large ground-floor niche shows St Michael triumphing over the devil while the highest niche is reserved for Christ.

Impressive interior A further depiction of the Archangel Michael forms the altarpiece of the soaring, three-storey-high altar erected by Sustris, Dietrich and Schwarz (1586–9). However, the most dominant architectural feature is the triumphal arch at the entrance to the choir, symbolising the victory of the Counter-Reformation, echoed in the arches of the transepts, side chapels and galleries. The Royal Crypt contains the tombs of 41 members of the Wittelsbach family.

Michaelskirche has Europe's widest vault (20m) outside of Rome

HIGHLIGHTS

- High Altar
- *St Michael fighting the Devil*, Christoph Schwarz
- Four bronze reliefs, Hubert Gerhard
- Royal and Jesuit Crypts
- Reliquary shrine of Saints Cosmos and Damian
- *Mary Magdalen at the feet of Christ Crucified*, Giovanni da Bologna
- *Annunciation*, Peter Candid

INFORMATION

- ✚ N23
- ✉ Neuhauser Strasse 52
- ☎ 231 70 60
- 🕐 Royal Crypt: Mon–Fri 10–4.30, Sat 10–1
- 🚇 U- or S-Bahn Karlsplatz
- ♿ None
- 🚋 Tram 17, 18, 19, 20, 21 27
- ↔ Frauenkirche (➤ 36)

ASAMKIRCHE

HIGHLIGHTS

- *Gnadenstuhl (Throne of Mercy)*, Ä G Asam
- Ceiling fresco, C D Asam
- Two-tiered High Altar
- Wax effigy of St John Nepomuk
- Statues of John the Baptist and St John the Evangelist
- Portraits of the Asam Brothers
- Façade

INFORMATION

- ✚ N23
- ✉ Sendlinger Strasse 62
- 🕐 Daily 8–5:30
- Ⓜ U-Bahn Sendlinger Tor
- 🚋 Tram 17, 18, 20, 21, 27; bus 31, 56
- ♿ None
- ↔ Munich City Museum (▶ 35) Münchner Marionettentheater (▶ 80)

"The Asamkirche is perhaps Munich's finest example of rococo architecture. The narrow but sensational façade provides a mere hint of the sumptuous interior – one of the most lavish works of the celebrated Asam brothers."

The Asam brothers In 1729, master architect and sculptor Ägid Quirin Asam acquired a house in Sendlingerstrasse and built his own private church next door, assisted by his brother, a distinguished fresco artist. For this reason, the Church of St John Nepomuk (a Bohemian saint popular in 18th-century Bavaria) is better known as the Asamkirche. Even though Asam financed the construction, he was forced to open it to the public and the church was consecrated in 1746. Free from the normal constraints of a patron's demands, the brothers created a dazzling jewel of rococo architecture.

Lavish decoration Entering through the unobtrusive marble façade with its unusual plinth of unhewn rocks and the kneeling figure of St John Nepomuk, you will be immediately struck by the breathtaking opulence of the tiny, dark interior, crammed with sculptures, murals and gold leaf, and crowned by a magnificent ceiling fresco depicting the life of the saint. The long narrow nave, with its encircling gallery and projecting moulded cornice carries your eye straight to the glorious two-tiered high altar and shrine of St John Nepomuk. The gleaming gallery altar, portraying the Trinity and lit by an oval window representing the sun, is crowned by Ägid Quirin's *Throne of Mercy*, depicting Christ crucified, in the arms of God, wearing the papal crown.

12

MÜNCHNER STADTMUSEUM

❝Munich's unique, lively, eclectic person-ality is reflected in the diverse nature of the City Museum's collections, ranging from weapons and armour, fashion and fairgrounds to Biedermeier and films.❞

City history If your itinerary does not allow enough time to explore all the old parts of the city on foot, you should head straight to the History of the City section on the first floor. Exhibits here trace Munich's develop-ment since the Middle Ages through maps, models and extraordinary before-and-after photographs, illustrating the devastating effects of bombing during World War II.

Unusual collections As the museum is housed in the former city armoury, it is only fitting that it should contain one of the largest collections of ancient weaponry in Germany. Other collections worth visiting include fashion from the 18th century to the present, the second-largest musical instru-ment collection in Europe, and the German Brewery Museum, which traces the history of Germany's national drink. Don't miss the greatest treasure – Erasmus Grasser's 10 *Morris Dancers* (1480), magnificent examples of late Gothic secular art, originally carved for the Old Town Hall (➤ 39).

For children of all ages Everyone loves the Marionette Theatre Collection (Münchner Marionettentheater) on the third floor, one of the largest in the world, reflecting Bavaria's importance in the production of glove-puppets, shadow plays and mechani-cal toys. Following on from this is a rare and most enjoyable fairground museum. Look out for the moving King Kong!

HIGHLIGHTS

● History of Munich Museum
● Puppet Theatre and Fairground Museum
● Photography and Film Museum

Puppet in the City Museum

INFORMATION

🛈 N23
✉ St-Jakobs-Platz 1
☎ 233 223 70
🕐 Tue–Sun 10–5; late night Wed until 8:30
🍴 Café and beer garden (£)
Ⓜ U-Bahn Sendlinger Tor, U- and S-Bahn Marienplatz
🚌 Bus 52, 56
♿ Good
💷 Moderate
↔ Asamkirche (➤ 34), Münchner Marionettentheater (➤ 80)
❓ Tours, lectures

35

FRAUENKIRCHE

HIGHLIGHTS

- Gothic stained-glass windows
- *The Baptism of Christ*, Friedrich Pacher altarpiece
- Jan Polack altar panels
- *The Assumption*, Peter Candid
- St Lantpert's Chapel with wood figures of apostles and prophets from the workshop of Erasmus Grasser
- Princes' Vault

"This massive, brick-built late Gothic church symbolises Munich more than any other building. Its sturdy twin towers (99m and 100m high), with their Italian-Renaissance onion domes, dominate the city's skyline."

Munich's cathedral The Frauenkirche, built between 1468 and 1488, has been the cathedral of Southern Bavaria since 1821. Reconstructed from the rubble of World War II, little remains of the original design except the basic architectural elements and the windows in the choir. Its strength lies in its simplicity and awesome proportions, making it the largest reconstructed medieval building in Munich.

The Frauenkirche's twin onion-domed spires

Onion-domes Thirty years after the church's consecration, the towers were still roofless. In 1524, unique green Italian-Renaissance onion-domes were erected as a temporary measure. This eccentric addition to the existing unembellished structure was once irreverently described as resembling two beer mugs with lids! However, the domes became so popular that they were retained.

INFORMATION

- ✚ N23
- ✉ Frauenplatz 1
- ☎ 290 08 20
- 🕐 South Tower: Apr–Oct, Mon–Sat 10–5
- Ⓤ U- or S-Bahn Marienplatz
- 🚋 Tram 19; bus 52
- ♿ None
- ↔ New Town Hall (➤ 37), Toy Museum (➤ 39)

The Devil's Footprint A footprint is visible in the stone floor near the entrance. Legend has it that the Devil visited the church and stamped his foot in delight because the architect had apparently forgotten to put in windows, though the building was flooded with light. Jörg von Halsbach's ingenious design meant that no windows were visible from this point, thus giving *him* the last laugh.

14

NEUES RATHAUS

"Eleven o'clock is the magic hour for tourists who crowd Marienplatz to see the world-famous Munich Glockenspiel in action – without doubt the main attraction of the New Town Hall for me. It's also a great place to people-watch."

Towers and turrets The imposing New Town Hall, seat of the city government for nearly a century, dominates the entire north side of Marienplatz, and is traditionally the scene of tournaments, festivals and ceremonies. Constructed between 1867 and 1909 around six courtyards with towers and turrets, sculptures and gargoyles, its neo-Gothic style was at the time still controversial, but the Neues Rathaus has since become one of Munich's landmarks.

The Glockenspiel The main front of the building is decorated with figures of Bavarian royalty alongside saints and characters from local folklore. The central tower viewing platform offers a fantastic view of the city centre, and houses one of the largest Glockenspiels (carillons) in Europe. This massive mechanical clock, boasting 43 bells, plays four different tunes while 32 almost life-sized carved figures present scenes from Munich's history: the jousting match at the marriage of Duke Wilhelm V with Renate of Lorraine in 1568, and the *Schäfflertanz* (Coopers' dance) of 1517, celebrating the end of the Black Death. This dance is still re-enacted in Munich's streets every seven years (next in 1998). Both Glockenspiel events can be seen daily at 11 in the morning, and also at noon and 5 in summer. The cuckoo ending the performance never fails to bring a smile.

HIGHLIGHTS

- Glockenspiel
- Façade
- Tower
- Ratskeller (➤ 63)

INFORMATION

- ✚ N24
- ✉ Marienplatz
- ☎ 233 03 00
- ◷ Tower: Mon–Fri 9–7; weekends 10–7; winter, daily 9–4:30
- 🍴 Ratskeller beer hall and restaurant (££)
- Ⓤ U- or S-Bahn Marienplatz
- 🚌 Bus 52
- ♿ Few
- 💷 Admission to tower DM3
- ↔ Frauenkirche (➤ 36), Peterskirche (➤ 38), Toy Museum (➤ 39), Viktualienmarkt (➤ 40)
- ❓ The public is admitted to council meetings by prior arrangement (☎ 233 65 77)

PETERSKIRCHE

HIGHLIGHTS

- High Altar (Nikolaus Stuber, Ägid Quirin Asam and Erasmus Grasser)
- Clock tower
- Schrenk Altar
- Jan Polack's five Gothic pictures
- Mariahilf Altar (Ignaz Günther)
- Corpus-Christi Altar (Ignaz Günther)
- Aresinger-Epitaph (Erasmus Grasser)

INFORMATION

- ✠ N24
- ✉ Petersplatz
- ☎ 260 48 28
- ◎ Tower: Mon–Sat 9–6; Sun 10–6. Closed in bad weather
- ⬚ U- or S-Bahn Marienplatz
- ⬚ Bus 52
- ♿ None
- ⬚ Tower: DM2.50
- ⬌ New Town Hall (➤ 37), Toy Museum (➤ 39), Viktualienmarkt (➤ 40)

❝*The Peterskirche is the oldest parish church in the city, known affectionately to Münchners as 'Alter Peter'. It has been immortalised in a traditional song which claims 'Until Old Peter's tower falls down, we'll have a good life in Munich town'.*❞

A chequered history The Peterskirche dates from the foundations of the city itself in 1158, on a slight hill called the 'Petersbergl', where the monks (who gave their name to Munich) had established a settlement in the 11th century. Its original Romanesque structure was expanded in Gothic style, and later remodelled along Renaissance lines in the 17th century, when the famous tower with its characteristic lantern dome was created.

The church was almost entirely destroyed during World War II. In an attempt to restore the church to its former glory, Bavarian Radio stirred the hearts of the people of Munich by playing only a shortened version of the 'Alter Peter' song, and public donations flowed in. The full version was at last heard again on 28 October 1951, once the tower had been completed.

The bells, the bells The most extraordinary feature of the tower is its eight asymmetrically placed clock-faces, designed so that, according to Munich comedian Karl Valentin, eight people can tell the time at once. The best time to hear Alter Peter's famous chimes, including one of the largest bells in Germany, is at 3 on a Saturday afternoon, ringing in the Sabbath. The 306-step climb to the viewing platform is rewarded by a dramatic bird's-eye view of Munich with its magnificent Alpine backdrop.

SPIELZEUGMUSEUM (TOY MUSEUM)

❝*Munich's Old Town Hall with its romantic Gothic façade of turrets and towers provides a fairy-tale setting for a unique collection of antique toys. This museum will delight children and evoke happy childhood memories for adults.***❞**

Toys galore It would be quite easy to miss the tiny entrance to the Toy Museum, hidden at the foot of the Altes Rathaus' (Old Town Hall's) grand tower in the southeast corner of Marienplatz. From here, a narrow spiral staircase leads up the Gothic tower to four floors of neatly arranged European and American toys dating from the last two centuries – a nostalgic collection of teddy bears, toy soldiers, model cars and dolls belonging to local caricaturist Ivan Steiger.

It is best to begin at the top and work your way down the tower in order to trace the history of toys, starting with the oldest dolls, animals and folk toys, dating back to 1780, from Bohemia, Vienna, Russia and other famous European toy-making centres. Make sure you don't miss the smallest doll in the world and the celebrated Steiff bears.

Lower down the tower, a splendid collection of carousels and steam engines is followed by part of the Hauser-Elastolin archive collection (one of Germany's main toy producers), and a series of American toys made famous here through comics, including Felix the Cat, Humpty Dumpty and other childhood favourites. The second floor contains a series of sophisticated model railways, while the first floor has a fine collection of dolls and dolls' houses.

Clock on the Old Town Hall

HIGHLIGHTS

- Steiff teddy bears
- Hauser-Elastolin collection
- Smallest doll in the world
- Folk toys from Berchtesgaden
- Jumping jacks from Oberammergau
- Moscovian painted puppets
- Model Zeppelin
- First ever Bakelite toy television

INFORMATION

- ✚ N24
- ✉ Im Alten Rathausturm
- ☎ 29 40 01
- ⏰ daily 10–5.30
- Ⓤ U- or S-Bahn Marienplatz
- 🚌 Bus 52
- ♿ None
- 💷 Admission DM5/DM1
- ↔ New Town Hall (➤ 37), Peterskirche (➤ 38), Viktualienmarkt (➤ 40)

39

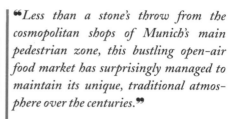

VIKTUALIENMARKT

Viktualienmarkt's maypole

HIGHLIGHTS

- Valentin Museum (► 55)
- Rottler – over 40 different kinds of potato
- Edgar's Müsli-Eck – muesli dishes (► 69)
- Lebkuchen Schmidt – spiced biscuits (► 73)
- Münchner Suppenküche – soup kitchen (► 69)
- Nordseefisch – fish snacks (► 69)
- Pferdemetzger – speciality horsemeat sausages
- Kräuterstand Freisinger – herbs and spices
- Honighäusl – herbal honey wines

INFORMATION

- ✚ N24
- 🕐 Mon–Fri 7:30–6; Sat 7:30–1
- 🍴 Numerous stands serve hot and cold snacks (£)
- Ⓤ U- or S-Bahn Marienplatz
- 🚌 Bus 52
- ↔ New Town Hall (► 37), Peterskirche (► 38), Toy Museum (► 39)

"Less than a stone's throw from the cosmopolitan shops of Munich's main pedestrian zone, this bustling open-air food market has surprisingly managed to maintain its unique, traditional atmosphere over the centuries."

A long tradition In 1807 it was decided that the market in Marienplatz had become too small for the rapidly growing trade. The foundation stone for a new Viktualienmarkt was laid in a grassy field outside the city, where livestock grazed and stage-coaches stopped. Today the site boasts Munich's oldest, largest and most attractive market with quaint green wooden stalls and colourful striped umbrellas.

Open-air delicatessen The lively atmosphere of the market owes much to the robust market women, famous for their loud and colourful abuse. Dare to haggle over the price or quality here and you will be scolded in an earthy Bavarian dialect you won't understand, but you'll get the message! Their top-quality products are expensive but offer the discerning shopper a vast range of fresh produce ranging from Bavarian blue cheese to Alpine herbs and flowers. Look out for seasonal produce, including neatly tied bundles of asparagus and mountains of freshly picked cranberries in summer.

Open-air restaurant Try some Bavarian specialities from the little taverns and stands dotted around the market – *Leberkäs* (meat loaf) or a *Brat-* or *Weisswürst* (sausage); wash it down with a typically Bavarian *Weissbier* in the beer garden set up around the maypole, the scene of lively May Day celebrations.

ODEONSPLATZ

"Situated at the start of Munich's two finest boulevards, this spacious square is surrounded by monumental buildings steeped in history and tradition. Rubbing the noses of the lions guarding the entrance to the Residenz brings good luck."

Grand plan for urban expansion Ludwig I entrusted the layout of Odeonsplatz to Leo von Klenze in the early 19th century, to demonstrate the wealth of his flourishing kingdom. It also shows Klenze's passion for Renaissance Italy. His neo-classical Leuchtenberg-Palais (today the Bavarian Ministry of Finance) was modelled on the Palazzo Farnese in Rome, and set the pattern for the development of the magnificent Ludwigstrasse.

Apart from the striking Theatinerkirche (➤ 57), Bavaria's first baroque building, and for many the most beautiful church in Munich, perhaps the most imposing building in Odeonsplatz is the Feldherrnhalle (Military Commanders' Hall), commissioned by Ludwig I as a tribute to the Bavarian army, and adorned with statues of Bavarian generals. Note the faces of the two bronze lions; one is said to be growling at the Residenz while the other, facing the church, remains silent.

The Court Garden The peaceful Hofgarten beside Odeonsplatz is laid out in its original 17th-century Italian plan of beautifully tended flowerbeds and fountains. The garden is enclosed on two sides by long arcades housing galleries and cafés, and by the impressive Staatskanzlei building to the east (➤ 59).

HIGHLIGHTS

- Theatinerkirche (➤ 57)
- Feldherrnhalle
- Hofgarten
- Leuchtenberg-Palais
- Odeon
- Ludwig I monument
- Preysing Palais
- Staatskanzlei (➤ 59)

INFORMATION

- ⊞ N24
- 🍴 Hofgarten Café (££)
- Ⓤ U-Bahn Odeonsplatz
- 🚌 Bus 53
- ↔ Residenz (➤ 42), House of Art (➤ 46), English Garden (➤ 47)

Theatinerkirche, burial place of the Wittelsbachs

19

RESIDENZ

The splendid ceiling of the Antiquarium

INFORMATION

- 🞣 N24
- ✉ Residenzstrasse/Max-Joseph-Platz
- ☎ 29 06 71
- 🕐 Tue–Sun 10–4:30
- 🚇 U- or S-Bahn Marienplatz, U-Bahn Odeonsplatz
- 🚋 Tram 19; bus 53
- ♿ Good
- 🎟 Admission DM5
- ↔ Odeonsplatz (➤ 41), Nationaltheater ➤ 44)
- ❓ Tours daily: rooms 1–81 (morning), rooms 82–112 (afternoon). Separate tour for the Schatzkammer

"It is easy to imagine the Wittelsbachs' glorious heyday in the glittering state rooms of this magnificent palace, built to demonstrate the power and wealth of five centuries of dukes, prince–electors and kings – an absolute treasure trove."

Historical evolution Despite devastating damage in World War II, the Residenz was painstakingly reconstructed over four decades. Now it is possible to see it restored to its original state: a harmonious fusion of Renaissance, baroque, rococo and neo-classical styles. As you explore the 112 grand rooms crammed with priceless treasures, you can trace the centuries of architectural development, as well as the history and life-styles of the great Wittelsbach dynasty.

Palace highlights It would take a day to see the palace, so limit your tour to the following: the Ahnengalerie (Ancestral Portrait Gallery), with 121 members of the Wittelsbach family; the Hofkapelle and Reiche Kapelle – two intimate chapels, one for the courtiers and the other for the royal family; the Brunnenhof courtyard with its magnificent fountain; the unusual shell-encrusted Grottenhof courtyard; and the Antiquarium, the largest Renaissance vaulted hall in northern Europe.

Jewel in the crown The Cuvilliés Theatre, jewel of the Residenz and the finest rococo theatre in the world, is a truly dazzling spectacle. Built in 1750, it witnessed the première of Mozart's *Idomeneo* in 1781. Visit the Treasury (Schatzkammer) to see the crown jewels and one of the most valuable collections of ecclesiastical and secular treasures in Europe, spanning a thousand years.

20

HOFBRÄUHAUS

❝ *No trip to Munich is complete without a visit to the Hofbräuhaus despite its being a tourist honeypot. In summer I prefer to sip my cool beer in the shady courtyard, although the beer hall is more fun.* ❞

Royal beer The Hofbräuhaus was founded by Wilhelm V in 1589 to produce a special dark ale for his court, because he disliked the expensive local beer. Beer in Bavaria had been considered an aristocratic drink ever since the harsh winters of the 14th century destroyed the Bavarian vineyards. The ordinary citizens of Munich were unable to taste this royal brew until 1828 when the brewery finally became an inn.

The Battle of the Hofbräuhaus The first mass meeting of the National Socialist Workers' Party (later the Nazi Party) was held in the Hofbräuhaus in 1920. It soon became regarded as the city's most prestigious political beer-hall arena. Here Hitler established himself as a powerful orator. On 4 November 1921, his storm troops first gained notoriety here in a huge brawl, later known as the *Schlacht* (Battle) *im Hofbräuhaus*. Despite the hurling of chairs and beer mugs, Hitler managed to finish his speech.

World's Most Famous Pub Undoubtedly the city's best-known institution after the Oktoberfest, and a superb meeting place for visitors from all over the world, the Hofbräuhaus – with its long tables, buxom *Dirndl*-clad waitresses and jolly Bavarian music – is a must for tourists, if only to join in with the popular drinking song '*In München steht ein Hofbräuhaus, eins, zwei, g'soffa*' ... 'one, two and down the hatch'!

DID YOU KNOW?

Bock beer test
In the Hofbräuhaus, that refuge of Bavarian culture, the 'bock test' was at one time used as a quality check. Fresh May bock beer was poured onto a wooden bench. Hard-headed beer drinkers would sit on this bench drinking bock beer for several hours, allowing nature to take its course there and then! If the bench stuck to their backsides when they all got up, then the beer was considered good – if not, then it was too thin.

INFORMATION

➕ N24
✉ Am Platzl 9
☎ 22 16 76 or 291 36 10
🕐 10–midnight. Brass band from 11AM
🚇 U- or S-Bahn Marienplatz
🚊 Tram 19, Bus 52
♿ Good

21

NATIONALTHEATER

INFORMATION

- N24
- Max-Joseph-Platz 2
- 21 85 19 20
- Box office: Mon–Fri 10–1, 3:30–5:30; Sat 10–12:30
- U-or S-Bahn Marienplatz, U-Bahn Odeonsplatz
- Tram 19; bus 52, 53
- Few
- DM5 for tour
- Odeonsplatz (➤ 41), Residenz (➤ 42)
- Tickets available in advance at the box office (☎ 2 13 16) in Maximilianstrasse 11, or from the theatre itself one hour before the performance. Guided tours on Fridays at 2PM (except during August and September)

"*Munich's Nationaltheater ranks among the world's leading opera-houses. It is one of the few German theatres to have been restored to its magnificent pre–war splendour and is definitely worth a visit, even if opera is not your scene.*"

People's opera-house The Nationaltheater has been home to the world famous Bayerische Staatsoper (Bavarian State Opera) for nearly two centuries – a distinguished Greek-temple design with a simple colonnaded façade which, after wartime bombing, stood in ruins for years until a group of citizens raised sufficient funds (DM63 million) to restore it to its former glory. It was reopened in 1963.

Behind the scenes Once a week on Fridays, during a fascinating tour, the general public are given the chance to take a rare glimpse backstage and to view the ingenious, high-tech stage machinery. The grandiose auditorium, with five tiers of seating decorated in plush red, gold, ivory and dove-blue, is crowned by an enormous chandelier which magically disappears into the roof when the curtain rises. The impressive 'Greek' rooms of the foyer provide an elegant setting for the audience to promenade in their finery.

Opening nights Many important operas have been premièred here over the centuries, including five Wagner operas during the reign of Ludwig II, and many eminent people have conducted, directed and performed here in a repertoire ranging from traditional Munich favourites – Mozart, Wagner and Strauss – to new commissions from living German composers.

DEUTSCHES MUSEUM

"If you spent one minute at each exhibit, 36 working days later you would have seen everything at this museum of superlatives – Munich's most famous, Germany's most visited and one of the world's biggest museums of science and technology."

Voyage of discovery In 1903, engineer Oskar von Miller founded the Museum of Masterworks of Science and Technology. Following his death, the collection moved to its present building on its own island on the Isar and was officially opened in 1925. Over the years it continued to grow and today, with over 17,000 exhibits ranging from the sundial to the space shuttle, the Deutsches Museum offers young and old alike a fascinating voyage of discovery.

Learning experience The most popular departments are mining (including a reconstructed coal-mine), computer science, the various transportation sections and the Planetarium. Everything has been designed for your comfort and enjoyment; alongside original examples are audio-visual displays, experiments and hands-on models.

Unique exhibits Dramatic displays include star shows at the Planetarium, an ear-splitting high voltage demonstration (a 220,000-volt flash of lightning) and a vast model railway on the ground floor. Other highlights include the first German submarine; one of the first jet planes; Karl Benz's first car; and the bench on which Otto Hahn proved the splitting of the atom.

HIGHLIGHTS

- Planetarium
- Faraday's Cage and high-voltage demonstration
- First German submarine
- Karl Benz's *Automobil Nummer I*
- Copy of the 'Puffing Billy' steam train
- Reconstruction of a coal-mine
- Reconstruction of the prehistoric caves at Lascaux
- Dornier DO 31 and Junkers JU52 aircraft
- 19th-century sailing ship – 60m long – the biggest exhibit

INFORMATION

✚	024
✉	Auf der Isarinsel
☎	21 79 433
◷	Daily 9–5
🍴	Restaurant (££), railroad-carriage café (£)
Ⓢ	S-Bahn Isartor
🚃	Tram 18
♿	Excellent
💷	Admission DM9

HAUS DER KUNST (HOUSE OF ART)

HIGHLIGHTS

- *Waste with John F Kennedy, Eduardo Paolozzi, 1971/85*
- *Self-portrait, Andy Warhol, 1967*
- *'I know how you must feel, Brad', Roy Lichtenstein, 1963*
- *Grosses Stilleben mit Fernrohr, Max Beckmann, 1927*
- *Sitting Woman, Pablo Picasso, 1941*
- *Large Sedona-frieze, Max Ernst, 1948*
- *Meine Mutter, meine Mutter, meine Mutter, Salvador Dali, 1929*
- *Improvisation, Wassily Kandinsky, 1910*
- *Nordermühle, Emil Nolde, 1932*
- *Der Tod, Ernst Barlach, 1925*

INFORMATION

- 🎫 M24
- ✉ Prinzregentenstrasse 1
- ☎ 21 12 71 37
- 🕐 Tue–Sun 10–5; Thu till 8
- 🍴 Café (£)
- 🚇 U-Bahn Odeonsplatz or Lehel
- 🚊 Tram 17; bus 53
- ♿ Good
- 💵 DM6. Sun and hols free
- ↔ English Garden (➤ 47), Bavarian National Museum (➤ 48)

" *This monstrous Nazi building was nick-named the 'Weisswurst' (white sausage) gallery by Hitler's opponents, because of its crude neo-classical columns. Inside, however, you will find one of Germany's finest museums of modern art.* **"**

Degenerate art Immediately after seizing power in 1933, Adolf Hitler ordered the construction of a 'House of German Art' (Haus der Kunst). It was opened in 1937 by Joseph Goebbels, Reichsminister of Prop-aganda, at the time of the notorious *Entartete Kunst* (Degenerate Art) exhibition at the Hofgarten which ridiculed contemporary avant-garde artists such as Klee, Dix and Beckmann who were henceforth banned by the Nazi regime. There is a pleasing irony in the fact that today the pictures on display are largely the work of those 'degenerate' artists (who continued to paint in secret) and are now recognised as being among the great classics of modern art.

Fine art The east and central sections of the Haus der Kunst are popular venues for temporary exhibitions of modern art, but the main gallery, housing the Staatsgalerie Moderner Kunst (Bavarian State Gallery of Modern Art), is located in the west wing. Of the 450 paintings, sculptures and objects on display, around half are by German artists including Nolde, Kirchner, Kiefer, Baselitz. and Schlemmer. Alongside, you will find works by all the modern masters embracing expressionism, cubism, constructivism, mini-malism and abstract art, with rooms dedicated to Picasso, Klee, Munch, Braque and Dalí. More recent times are represented by a collection of American abstract and pop art.

ENGLISCHER GARTEN

" *There's nothing I enjoy more than walk-ing in this vast, idyllic park on a sunny day, whatever the season. The English Garden ranks highly on every Münchner's list of favourite city spots.* **"**

Munich's 'green lung' Stroll through the park and you will see people from all walks of life enjoying themselves here; families boating, musicians busking, children feeding the ducks, New Age groups gathered by the Love Temple, professionals picnicking in their lunch break, jolly crowds in the packed beer gardens. This is Munich's beloved 'green lung' – 373 hectares of parkland stretching over 5km along the River Isar, and one of the largest city parks in the world.

English influences The English Garden was created by Count Rumford and Ludwig von Sckell in 1789. Breaking away from the French style of manicured lawns and geomet-rical flowerbeds, they transformed the Wittelsbach hunting ground into an informal, countrified *Volksgarten* (people's park).

Attractions Start at the Kleinhesseloher See, an artificial lake with boats for hire. Or spend time relaxing at the Seehaus beer garden before heading south towards the Monopteros, a circular, Greek-style love temple with a splendid view of the park and the distant spires of old Munich. As well as English and Greek influences, the park also has a distinctive oriental flavour with its Japanese Tea House and Chinese Tower. It also marks the city's most famous beer garden – popular for its brass band, old-fashioned children's merry-go-round and permanent Oktoberfest atmosphere.

HIGHLIGHTS

- Chinese Tower
- Kleinhesseloher See and Seehaus
- Monopteros
- Japanese Tea House (tea ceremonies on the second weekend of every month between May and October)
- Rumford House

INFORMATION

- ✚ M24–H27
- 🕐 Dawn to dusk
- 🍴 Chinese Tower beer garden (££), Seehaus restaurant (£££) and beer garden (££), Japanese Tea House (£££), Aumeister restaurant and beer garden (££) (➤ 50)
- 🚇 U-Bahn Odeonsplatz, Universität, Giselastrasse, Münchener Freiheit
- 🚊 Tram 17; bus 44, 54, 154
- ❓ Rowing boats for hire at the Kleinhesseloher See
- ↔ House of Art (➤ 46), Bavarian National Museum (➤ 48)

25

BAYERISCHES NATIONALMUSEUM

Top: Riemenschneider
woodcarving

HIGHLIGHTS

- Medieval model of Munich,
  J Sandtner
- Augsburg Weaving Room
- Tilman Riemenschneider
  sculptures
- Ivory collection
- Crib collection
- Flanders Tapestry Room
- Weaponry Room
- Closet from Palais
  Tattenbach
- 14th-century stained-glass
  windows

INFORMATION

"The Bavarian National Museum, one of Europe's leading museums of folk art, is sure to give you a real taste of Bavarian life over the centuries."

Wittelsbach treasures Thanks to the Wittelsbach rulers' passion for collecting works of art, this museum was founded in 1855 by Maximilian II and transferred to its present site in 1900. Even the building mirrors the various periods represented within the museum in a clever design by Gabriel von Seidl dating from 1900; the west wing is Romanesque, the east wing Renaissance, the tower baroque and the west end rococo. The interior is divided into two main collections – Folklore and Art History – providing a comprehensive survey of German cultural history, both sacred and secular, from the early Middle Ages to the present.

Folklore A series of rooms authentically decorated with rustic Bavarian furniture, glass, pottery and woodcraft provides a wonderful insight into the country life of bygone years. The museum is especially famous for its sculptures by Hans Leinberger, Ignaz Günther and Tilman Riemenschneider, and its substantial crib collection.

Art history This collection consists of a series of specialist departments including Bavarian *Trachten* (traditional costume), tapestries, stained glass, porcelain, jewellery, miniatures, armour, weaponry and the largest ivory collection in Europe. Anyone interested in seeing how Munich looked 500 years ago should study the medieval model of the city, created by master woodworker Jakob Sandtner, on the first floor.

MUNICH's *best*

BEER HALLS & BEER GARDENS

Useful beer garden jargon

You can take your own food to most beer gardens. Better still, try some traditional Bavarian *Brotzeit* (snacks, literally 'bread time'), including *Radi* (large white radishes), *Brez'n* (pretzel bread), *Obatzda* (a Camembert and chive spread), *Steckerlfisch* (smoked mackerel) and *Schweinshax'n* (pork knuckles). Wash it all down with a *Maß* (litre) of beer, a *Radler* (lemonade shandy) or a refreshing *Spezi* (coke and lemonade mix).

Enjoying a friendly drink in one of Munich's many beer gardens

See Top 25 Sights for
CHINESISCHER TURM (➤ 47)
HOFBRÄUHAUS (➤ 43)
SEEHAUS (➤ 47)
VIKTUALIENMARKT (➤ 40)

ALTE VILLA (➤ 53)

AUGUSTINER-KELLER
One of Munich's most traditional beer cellars, just a few minutes' walk from the main station. Its popular beer garden seats over 5,000.
➕ N23 ✉ Arnulfstrasse 52 ☎ 59 43 93 ⏰ 10AM–1AM 🚇 U- or S-Bahn Hauptbahnhof 🚊 Tram 17

AUMEISTER
Situated at the northern edge of the English Garden, this former huntsman's lodge, now a beer garden, makes a perfect place to end a pleasant walk along the river.
➕ H26 ✉ Sondermeierstrasse 1 ☎ 32 52 24 ⏰ 10AM–11PM 🚇 U-Bahn Freimann

BRÄUSTÜBERL WEIHENSTEPHAN
This former Benedictine monastery in Freising is said to contain the oldest brewery in the world, particularly famous for its *Korbinian* 'strong beer'.
➕ Off map to north ✉ Weihenstephanbrauerei, Freising ☎ (08161) 130 04 ⏰ 9–9 🚇 S-Bahn Freising

FLAUCHER
One of Munich's most popular and most scenic beer gardens beside the River Isar, somewhat off the tourist track. Families bring their own picnics and candles here in the evening.
➕ Q22 ✉ Isarauen 1 ☎ 723 26 77 ⏰ 10AM–11PM 🚇 U-Bahn Brudermühlstrasse

HACKERKELLER
Ox-on-the-spit is the house speciality here,

served to the accompaniment of traditional Bavarian music.

🚇 022 ✉ Theresienhöhe 4 ☎ 50 70 04 🕐 5PM–1AM 🚇 U-Bahn Theresienwiese

HIRSCHGARTEN

Munich's largest beer garden, seating 8,000, near Schloss Nymphenburg. Children love the deer enclosure and huge park.

🚇 M19 ✉ Hirschgartenallee 1 ☎ 17 25 91 🕐 10AM–11:30PM 🚌 Tram 17; Bus 41, 68, 83

KLOSTER ANDECHS (▶ 53)

MATHÄSER BIERSTADT

This typical Munich beer cellar contains over 4,500 seats, making it one of the largest pubs in the world.

🚇 N23 ✉ Bayerstrasse 5 ☎ 59 28 96 🕐 8AM–11:30pm 🚇 U- or S-Bahn Hauptbahnhof

Pub sign in Munich's old town

MAX-EMANUEL-BRAUEREI

Famous for its folk music, this tiny beer garden near the university is always crowded.

🚇 M24 ✉ Adalbertstrasse 33 ☎ 271 51 58 🕐 10AM–11PM 🚇 U-Bahn Universität

MENTERSCHWAIGE

Royalty used to drink at this ancient beer garden, which today serves excellent Bavarian food in a romantic setting high above the Isar.

🚇 T22 ✉ Menterschwaigstrasse 4 ☎ 64 07 32 🕐 11AM–10.30PM 🚌 Tram 15, 25

ROSENGARTEN IM WESTPARK

Enjoy a hillside view of thousands of roses while sipping your beer in a delightful park setting.

🚇 020 ✉ Westpark 🕐 11–11 🚇 U-Bahn Westpark 🚌 Bus 33

ST EMMERAMSMÜHLE

Largely populated by the smart set, this is the beer garden in which to see and be seen.

🚇 J27 ✉ St Emmeram 41 ☎ 95 39 71 🕐 11–11 🚌 Bus 37, 88, 89, 188

TAXISGARTEN

This quiet, shady spot near Schloss Nymphenburg is renowned for its spare ribs.

🚇 L21 ✉ Taxisstrasse 12 ☎ 95 39 71 🕐 11–10:30 🚌 Bus 83, 177

WALDWIRTSCHAFT GROSSHESSELOHE

A long-time favourite of Münchners, overlooking the Isar gorge and famous for its live jazz.

🚇 Off map to south ✉ Georg-Kalb-Strasse 3 ☎ 79 50 88 🕐 11am–10.30pm 🚇 S-Bahn Grosshesselohe Isartalbahnhof

An endangered species

Following local complaints about excessive noise in the Waldwirtschaft Grosshesselohe beer garden, in April 1995 the Bavarian High Court ruled that it must close at 9:30 rather than 11:30PM. Some 20,000 people unsuccessfully protested at the 'First Bavarian Beer Garden Revolution' in Marienplatz in May. Closing time has since been extended to 10.30PM by the Administration Court.

CELEBRATIONS

Beer tent at the Oktoberfest

The first Oktoberfest

Amid the heaving throng, the hefty beermaids, the kaleidoscopic fairground and the blast of brass bands in the packed beer-tents, it is easy to forget the origin of the Oktoberfest. It all began in 1810 with the wedding party of Crown Prince Ludwig and Princess Theresa – a lavish affair with horse-racing, shooting matches and a fair, but ironically no beer.

FASCHING
Fasching or Carnival – Munich's 'fifth season' – officially starts at 11:11AM on 11 November, but celebrations don't really get under way until a few weeks before Lent, when costumed revellers run riot in a dazzling array of carnival processions, street parties and balls, climaxing in a massive open-air party at the Viktualienmarkt (➤ 40) on Shrove Tuesday.

STRONG BEER SEASON (STARKBIERZEIT)
In the 17th century, Paulaner monks started to brew a special, nourishing beer with an alcoholic content of 6.7 per cent, which was consumed as 'liquid bread' during Lent. The Pope, fortunately not a great beer drinker, pronounced that it was a fitting penance for Lent. The public began to look forward to it each year, and the Strong Beer Festival was born, a tradition unique to Munich, best celebrated at the Salvatorkeller am Nockherberg during the three weeks leading up to Easter.

OKTOBERFEST
The biggest beer festival in the world starts on the third Saturday in September when the Lord Mayor taps open the first barrel with the cry 'O'zapft is' ('It's open') and the massive beer binge begins. In 1995 a staggering 5.5 million litres of beer, 775,000 chickens and 640,000 sausages were consumed by a record 7 million visitors.

CHRISTMAS MARKET (CHRISTKINDLMARKT)
There's a special magic about Munich's Christmas Market, with its tiny snow-capped wooden huts clustered around Marienplatz, sparkling with light and crammed with Christmas goodies, tree decorations and the beautifully carved cribs that are so famous in Bavaria. After buying your stocking-fillers, gather round the enormous, brightly lit Christmas tree for carols, *Glühwein* and warm gingerbread.

LAKES

See Top 25 Sights For
KLEINHESSELOHER SEE (► 47)

AMMERSEE

Ammersee, with its lake promenades, bustling boat sheds and sandy beaches, is set in lush green countryside at the heart of Munich's lake district, easily reached by S-Bahn. Highlights include a trip on Bavaria's oldest paddle-steamer, the artists' colony at Diessen, live jazz in the Alte Villa beer garden at Utting, and Kloster Andechs, one of Germany's most important pilgrimage destinations, famous worldwide for its centuries-old brewing tradition and *Andechser Bock* beer.

➕ Off map to southwest 🚇 S-Bahn Herrsching

FELDMOCHINGERSEE

This beach caters for handicapped people, with a machine to raise and lower swimmers into the water. What's more, the water is so clean you could almost drink it.

➕ Off map to north 🚇 S-Bahn Feldmoching

FERINGASEE

One of the most popular lakes near the city, with sandy beaches, and good for windsurfing.

➕ H29 🚇 S-Bahn Unterföhring

KARLSFELDER SEE

A great place to bring children, with safe swimming and excellent sports facilities. You might even catch a glimpse of Emil, the local 'Loch Ness' monster.

➕ Off map to northwest 🚇 S-Bahn Karlsfeld

STARNBERGER SEE

The Starnberger See's banks are still lined with the baroque palaces of Bavaria's aristocracy, and the area remains predominantly the domain of the rich and famous. Today, as the largest of the five lakes just south of the city and Munich's main summer playground, it offers many sporting activities – horse-riding, golf, swimming and sailing to name but a few – set against a breathtaking Alpine backdrop.

➕ Off map to southwest
🚇 S-Bahn Starnberg

Mysterious phenomena

While the Starnberger See is famed for its supposed sea monster – a giant worm which agitates the water even when there isn't a breath of wind – the Ammersee offers a curious, inexplicable phenomenon: a *Schaukelwelle* (rocking wave) which crosses the Ammersee from north to south and back again like a giant pendulum every 24 minutes, the water rising and falling about 10cm against the shore.

Boats for hire on the Ammersee

MUSEUMS & GALLERIES

Valentin's Day

Karl Valentin (1882–1948), Bavaria's answer to Charlie Chaplin, was loved for his quirky wit and misanthropic humour. He started out in beer halls but soon attracted the attention of Schwabing's intellectuals, including dramatist Bertolt Brecht. Perhaps best remembered for his sketch in which he put fish in a bird-cage and birds in an aquarium, his statue (along with those of other popular folk entertainers) can be seen today at the Viktualienmarkt (➤ 40).

See Top 25 Sights For
BAVARIAN NATIONAL MUSEUM (➤ 48)
BMW-MUSEUM (26)
DACHAU MEMORIAL MUSEUM (➤ 27)
DEUTSCHES MUSEUM (➤ 45)
HOUSE OF ART (➤ 46)
LENBACHHAUS (➤ 29)
MUNICH CITY MUSEUM (➤ 35)
NEW PICTURE GALLERY (➤ 32)
NYMPHENBURG PORCELAIN MUSEUM (➤ 24)
OLD PICTURE GALLERY (➤ 31)
TOY MUSEUM (39)

ERWIN VON KREIBIG GALLERY
Discover the latest trends in the Munich art scene with temporary exhibitions of promising local artists.
✚ L19 ✉ Südliches Schlossrondell 1, Schloss Nymphenburg ☎ 178 11 69 🕐 2–5. Closed Mon and Fri 🚊 Tram 12 💰 Cheap

FLUGWERFT SCHLEISSHEIM
A must for aeroplane buffs, this extension of the Deutsches Museum's aviation display is located on a disused airfield.
✚ Off map to north ✉ Effnerstrasse 18 ☎ 315 71 40 🕐 Daily 9–5 🚇 S-Bahn Oberschleissheim 💰 Moderate

GERMAN HUNTING AND FISHING MUSEUM
The most important collection of its kind in Germany, including the 'Wolpertinger', a 'hoax' animal resembling a marmot with webbed feet, antlers and wings, found only in Bavaria.
✚ N23 ✉ Neuhauser Strasse 33 ☎ 17 90 80 🕐 Daily 9:30–5; Mon and Thu until 9 🚇 U- or S-Bahn Marienplatz 💰 Moderate

GERMAN THEATRE MUSEUM
Germany's rich theatrical past is brought to life in this small but fascinating display of set designs, costumes, photographs and props.
✚ N24 ✉ Galeriestrasse 4 ☎ 22 24 49 🕐 Tue–Sun 10–4 🚇 U-Bahn Odeonsplatz 💰 Moderate

THE LABYRINTH – THE ALTERNATIVE PINAKOTHEK
A perfect introduction to classical and modern art.
✚ N25 ✉ Maria-Theresia-Strasse 14 ☎ 47 21 02 🕐 Wed–Sat 3–8; Sun 11–6 🚌 Bus 53 💰 Expensive

MÜNCHNER FEUERWEHRMUSEUM
Interesting museum with exciting videos showing the latest fire-fighting methods. Telephone first to avoid disappointment.
✚ 023 ✉ An der Hauptfeuerwache 8 ☎ 23 53 31 88 🕐 Sat 9–4 🚇 U-Bahn Sendlinger Tor

MUSEUM VILLA STUCK
This stunning *Jugendstil* villa, the former home of Franz von Stuck, has been beautifully restored and contains changing exhibitions dedicated to turn-of-the-century art.
⊞ N25 ⊠ Prinzregentenstrasse 60 ☎ 45 55 51 25 🕐 Tue–Sun 10–5; Thu until 9 🚃 Tram 18; Bus 53 🚇 U-Bahn Prinzregentenplatz 💷 Cheap

PALAEONTOLOGY MUSEUM
Children find the dinosaurs, fossils and prehistoric trees on view here fascinating.
⊞ M23 ⊠ Richard-Wagner-Strasse 10 ☎ 52 03 361 🕐 Mon–Thu 8–4; Fri 8–2, first Sun in month 10–4 🚇 U-Bahn Königsplatz 💷 Free

SCHACK-GALERIE
The artistic spirit of 19th-century German art is captured in this intimate gallery.
⊞ N25 ⊠ Prinzregentenstrasse 9 ☎ 238 05 224 🕐 Wed–Mon 10–5 🚃 Tram 18; Bus 53 🚇 U-Bahn Prinzregentenplatz 💷 Cheap

SIEMENS-MUSEUM
Discover what the future holds in electrical and electronic engineering, described for the layman.
⊞ N23 ⊠ Prannerstrasse 10 ☎ 234 26 60 🕐 Mon–Fri 9–5; Sun 10–5 🚇 U- or S-Bahn Karlsplatz 🚃 Tram 19 💷 Free

VALENTIN-MUSEUM
Showcase for eccentric humour of Munich's Karl Valentin, with oddities including his first snow-sculpture 'now unfortunately melted'. Bizarre opening times too.
⊞ N24 ⊠ Im Isartor ☎ 22 32 66 🕐 Mon, Tue, Fri, Sat 11:01–5:29; Sun 10:01–5:29 & Café (££) 🚇 S-Bahn Isartor 💷 Cheap

ZAM (CENTRE FOR EXTRAORDINARY MUSEUMS)
Munich's most unusual collections – chamber pots, pedal cars, pad-locks and even Easter bunnies.
⊞ N24 ⊠ Westen-riederstrasse 41 ☎ 290 41 21 🕐 Daily 10–6 🚇 S-Bahn Isartor 💷 Expensive

City of art
Munich claims to be one of the richest European cities of art, thanks largely to the Wittelsbach family, the ambitious rulers of Munich who avidly collected priceless works of art for over 650 years. The majority of the hundred or so museums and galleries in town offer free entrance on Sundays and the Tourist Office produces a useful *Official Monthly Programme of Events* with up-to-date information on current exhibitions.

Above: Der Olymp, *by Jenssens, New Picture Gallery*
Left: Heilige Barbara, *Bavarian National Museum*

55

CASTLES & CHURCHES

Lovers' rendezvous

Schloss Blutenburg (above) is an undeniably romantic castle and was originally built as a love-nest for Agnes Bernauer by her secret lover Duke Albrecht III in 1438. Sadly, their romance never had much of a chance to flourish as, shortly after completion of the magical castle, she was accused of being a witch and was drowned in the Danube at Straubing.

See Top 25 Sights For
ASAMKIRCHE (▶34)
FRAUENKIRCHE (▶36)
PETERSKIRCHE (▶38)
RESIDENZ (▶42)
SCHLEISSHEIM PALACES (▶28)
SCHLOSS NYMPHENBURG (▶24)

ASAM-SCHLÖSSL 'MARIA EINSIEDEL'
This once ordinary house was transformed into a royal country residence in the early 18th century with a magnificent façade painted by Cosmas Damian Asam. Today it is a restaurant.
✚ R21 ✉ Benediktbeurer Strasse 19 ⊙ Restaurant: 11AM–midnight Ⓠ U-Bahn Thalkirchen

DAMENSTIFTSKIRCHE ST ANNA
Only the ornate façade of St Anne's survived World War II and the church was rebuilt in the 1950s. The interior, decorated in pastel shades, contains stucco work and frescoes by the Asam brothers.
✚ N23 ✉ Damenstiftstrasse 1 Ⓠ U- or S-Bahn Karlsplatz

DREIFALTIGKEITSKIRCHE
The Church of the Holy Trinity was built in the early 18th century following the prophecies of a young Munich mystic who claimed that Divine Judgement was about to strike and the city could only be saved if an oath was taken to build a church. Curiously, it was one of the few churches undamaged during World War II.
✚ N23 ✉ Pacellistrasse 6 Ⓠ U- or S-Bahn Karlsplatz

HEILIGGEISTKIRCHE
The Gothic Church of the Holy Ghost, situated at the northern end of the Viktualienmarkt, is crammed full of religious treasures.
✚ N24 ✉ Tal 77 Ⓠ U- or S-Bahn Marienplatz

LUDWIGSKIRCHE

This elegant church contains the world's largest fresco after Michelangelo's *Last Judgement* in the Sistine Chapel. Peter Cornelius's *Last Judgement* took four years to complete.

✚ M24 ✉ Ludwigstrasse 20 🚇 U-Bahn Universität

SCHLOSS BLUTENBURG

An idyllic moated 15th-century castle and one-time Wittelsbach summer residence in Obermenzing with a chapel full of treasures. It also contains an international collection of children's books – the largest library of youth literature in the world with over 500,000 books in some 100 different languages.

✚ L16 ✉ Obermenzing ☎ 891 21 10 🕐 Chapel 10–5; library 11–6 🚆 S-Bahn Obermenzing ♿ Free admission to chapel and library

SCHLOSS DACHAU

Only one wing remains of this popular 16th-century summer residence and hunting ground for Munich royals. Today it contains a folk museum and a café which serves the best gateaux in Munich.

✚ Off map to northwest ☎ 08131/87923 🕐 May–Sep, Sat–Sun 2–5 🍴 Café on premises (££) 🚆 S-Bahn Dachau ♿ Moderate

SCHLOSS FÜRSTENRIED

This baroque castle, scene of King Maximilian II's magnificent hunting parties, is aligned with the Frauenkirche 13km away. Sadly the view down the avenue of lime trees is now interrupted by a motorway.

✚ S18 ✉ Forst-Kasten-Allee 🚇 U-Bahn Basler Strasse

SCHLOSS SURESNES

After the collapse of the socialist republic in 1919, this 18th-century summer residence served as a hideaway for the writer and revolutionary Ernst Toller until his arrest here. It then became home to artist Paul Klee from 1919 to 1921.

✚ L24 ✉ Werneckstrasse 24 🚇 U-Bahn Münchener Freiheit

THEATINERKIRCHE

Considered by many to be the most beautiful church in Munich, with its brilliant yellow façade (the first example of Bavarian baroque), the Theatinerkirche became an important architectural model for later Bavarian churches.

✚ N24 ✉ Theatinerstrasse 🚇 U-Bahn Odeonsplatz

A birthday church

The Court Church of St Kajetan was originally built to celebrate the birth of a son and heir to Princess Henriette Adelaide and Elector Ferdinand Maria, and their joy is mirrored in the lavish interior ornamentation, modelled on San Andrea del Valle in Rome. The church was assigned to the monks of the Theatine order, hence the name Theatinerkirche.

The Theatinerkirche

STATUES & FOUNTAINS

A full purse

There was once a fish market beside Konrad Knoll's famous Fish Fountain (1865) in Marienplatz. It then became the scene of the traditional 'Butcher's Leap' where butchers' apprentices were 'baptised' into the profession. Today, they say that if you wash your purse here on Ash Wednesday, it will never be empty. Indeed, the Lord Mayor keeps this custom alive, washing the City Purse here every year.

The Brunnenbuberl

See Top 25 Sights For
BRUNNENHOF FOUNTAIN, RESIDENZ (➤ 42)

ANGEL OF PEACE
This gleaming, golden figure, perched high above the River Isar, was built for the 25th anniversary of Germany's victory over France in 1871.
N25 ✉ Prinzregentenstrasse 🚌 Bus 53

BRUNNENBUBERL (FOUNTAIN BOY)
Public outcry greeted this naked young boy in 1895, but sculptor Mathias Gastiner refused to supply a fig leaf!
N23 ✉ Neuhauser Strasse 🚇 U- or S-Bahn Karlsplatz

CATTLE MARKET FOUNTAIN
Three cows mark this ancient marketplace, today a popular picnic spot.
N23 ✉ Rindermarkt 🚇 U- or S-Bahn Marienplatz

MARIENSÄULE
Marienplatz owes its name to this gracious figure of the Virgin Mary. All distances in Bavaria are measured from this point.
N23 ✉ Marienplatz 🚇 U- or S-Bahn Marienplatz

MONUMENT TO MAX-JOSEPH IV
Max Joseph, the first Wittelsbach king, wanted a more dignified standing pose but died before the statue was finished, so his son, Ludwig I, settled for this seated version.
N24 ✉ Max-Joseph-Platz 🚇 U- or S-Bahn Marienplatz

PUMUCKL FOUNTAIN
This cheeky character douses passers-by when they least expect it!
K23 ✉ Luitpold Park 🚇 U-Bahn Scheidplatz

STATUE OF BAVARIA
This famous lady representing Bavaria is 18m high. Climb the 112 steps inside for a splendid view from the top.
O22 ✉ Theresienwiese 🚇 U-Bahn Theresienwiese

WALKING MAN
Munich's newest sculpture (1995) by American sculptor, Jonathan Borofsky, is five storeys tall.
M24 ✉ Leopoldstrasse 36 🚇 U-Bahn Giselastrasse

WITTELSBACH FOUNTAIN
The two figures of Munich's loveliest neo-classical fountain (1895) symbolise the destructive and healing power of water.
N23 ✉ Lenbachplatz 🚇 U- or S-Bahn Karlsplatz

20TH-CENTURY ARCHITECTURE

See Top 25 Sights For
HOUSE OF ART (▶ 46)
NEW PICTURE GALLERY (▶ 32)
OLYMPIC PARK & VILLAGE (▶ 25)

BAVARIAN STATE CHANCELLERY

The gleaming glass and steel Staatskanzlei building is framed by a Renaissance arcade and has the dome of the former Army Museum as its centrepiece.

➕ N24 ✉ Hofgarten Ⓤ U-Bahn Odeonsplatz

BMW HEADQUARTERS

This giant, silver, four-cylinder building resembles a four-leaf clover. It was built between 1970 and 1972 by Viennese architect Karl Schwanzer to signal the company's technical orientation.

➕ J23 ✉ Petuelring 130 Ⓤ U-Bahn Petuelring

JUGENDSTILHAUS AINMILLERSTRASSE

Munich's first *Jugendstil* house (1900), recently restored to its original glory.

➕ L24 ✉ Ainmillerstrasse 22 Ⓤ U-Bahn Giselastrasse

KULTURZENTRUM GASTEIG

This striking combination of red brick and glass contains a high-tech concert hall, conservatory and municipal library.

➕ O25 ✉ Kellerstrasse 2–6 Ⓢ S-Bahn Isartor

MÜLLERSCHES VOLKSBAD (▶ 83)

MUNICH AIRPORT

Landing at the new Munich airport is rather like taking a voyage into the future. You could even be forgiven for thinking you were in a modern art gallery, with themes of light, space and movement used to counterbalance the more functional aspects of this unique construction.

➕ Off map to northeast ✉ Flughafen Ⓢ S-Bahn Flughafen

MUSIKHOCHSCHULE

Designed on Hitler's instruction by Paul Ludwig Troost, this 'Temple of Honour' (today the music academy) is connected to the Haus der Kulturinstitute opposite by an enormous wartime bunker system.

➕ M23 ✉ Arcisstrasse 12 Ⓤ U-Bahn Königsplatz

POST-UND-WOHNGEBÄUDE

One of Germany's most important buildings from the '20s, this post office-cum-apartment block has an unusual, elegantly curved façade.

➕ O22 ✉ Goetheplatz 1 Ⓤ U-Bahn Goetheplatz

'Hypo towers'

The 'new' post-war city contains a remarkable number of modern architectural gems. One of its most original recent wonders – the 114m Hypobank headquarters (above) – pierces the skyline in a striking series of shimmering glass and aluminium prisms, each of a different height and size. It was described by designers Walther and Bea Bentz as 'white sails billowing between silver masts'.

59

ATTRACTIONS FOR CHILDREN

Munich's very own 'Hollywood'

Children will love directing or starring in their own films, watching stuntmen in action and exploring familiar sets (even an entire Berlin street!) at the Bavaria Film Studios, location for many famous films including *Enemy Mine* and *The Never-Ending Story*. Munich has always had strong associations with the film industry, boasting a Film Museum (➤ 35), summer Film Festival, European Film College and a staggering 83 cinemas (➤ 77).

BAVARIA FILM STUDIOS

Glimpse behind the scenes of Europe's largest film studios, and learn the tricks of the trade.
✚ Off map to south ✉ Bavaria Filmplatz 7 ☎ 64 99 23 04 🕐 Mar–Oct 9–4 🚋 Tram 25 💷 Very expensive

CHILDREN'S THEATRES (➤ 80, 81)

CIRCUS KRONE

Munich's internationally acclaimed circus offers dazzling performances in its permanent 'big top' from December to March.
✚ M22 ✉ Marsstrasse 43 ☎ 55 81 66 🕐 Telephone for times 🚇 S-Bahn Hackerbrücke

FORUM DER TECHNIK

A high-tech entertainment centre containing Germany's first IMAX cinema (➤ 77) and the most modern planetarium in the world.
✚ 024 ✉ Museumsinsel 1 ☎ 2 11 25–1 80 🕐 10.30AM–10PM 🚇 S-Bahn Isartor 💷 Expensive

HELLABRUNN ZOO

The first 'Geo-Zoo' in the world (with animals grouped according to their regions).
✚ R22 ✉ Tierparkstrasse 30 ☎ 62 50 80 🕐 Apr–Sep 8–6; Oct–Mar 9–5 🚇 U-Bahn Thalkirchen 💷 Moderate

INTERNATIONAL YOUTH LIBRARY (➤ 57)

MUSEUM MENSCH UND NATUR

These hands-on displays show man's relationship with nature and the environment in an educational but fun way.

Steiff Teddy Bear (1907), Toy Museum

✚ L19 ✉ Schloss Nymphenburg ☎ 17 64 94 🕐 Tue–Sun 9–5. Closed public hols 🚋 Tram 12, 17; bus 41 💷 Cheap

NO-NAME-CITY

An entire Western Town with cowboys and Indians, gold-diggers and gamblers.
✚ Off map to east ✉ Gruberstrasse 60a, Poing ☎ 08121/7 96 66 🕐 Apr–Oct 9:30–6 (Sat till midnight) 🚇 S-Bahn Poing 💷 Very expensive

PALAEONTOLOGY MUSEUM (➤ 55)

MUNICH
where to...

SIX OF THE BEST

Prices

Expect to pay per person for a meal, excluding drink

£   up to DM25

££   up to DM50

£££   over DM50

Dining out

Eating and drinking in Bavaria, and especially in Munich, are major pastimes, with restaurants ranging from the culinary delights of Tantris and other gastronomic temples famous throughout Germany to quick snacks at a market *Imbiss* (snack-bar). Restaurants and cafés are often open all day (unless otherwise stated). Service is usually included in the price, although a small tip is welcomed.

BOGENHAUSER HOF (£££)

This small countrified restaurant is located in a traditional-style picture-book house which stands alone in a pretty garden. Reservations are essential if you wish to sample the inspired French-style cuisine and attentive service, as its close proximity to the Maximilaneum makes it a popular haunt for members of Parliament.
⊞ M25 ⊠ Ismaninger Strasse 85 ☎ 98 55 86 🕐 Closed Sun 🚋 Tram 18

GLOCKENBACH (£££)

Dine in style amid wood-panelled walls hung with modern art at this restaurant in the Glockenbach area of the city. The cuisine is top-class with no unnecessary frills.
⊞ 024 ⊠ Kapuzinerstrasse 29 ☎ 53 40 43 🕐 Mon – Sat lunch and dinner 🚇 U-Bahn Goetheplatz

HALALI (£££)

The secret of Halali's success is its old Bavarian style and good, unpretentious, regional home cooking, which includes a tempting range of game dishes. Try the tender venison in a juniper berry sauce with cranberries and wild mushrooms.
⊞ M24 ⊠ Schönfeldstrasse 22 ☎ 28 59 09 🕐 Mon–Fri lunch and dinner; Sat dinner only 🚇 U-Bahn Odeonsplatz

KÄFER-SCHÄNKE (£££)

This warren of elegant rooms situated above the famous Käfer delicatessen promises a gastronomic experience with creative dishes and a lavish buffet. A meal here is well worth the expense.
⊞ N25 ⊠ Schumannstrasse 1 ☎ 416 81 🕐 Mon–Sat noon–midnight 🚇 U-Bahn Prinzregentenplatz

KÖNIGSHOF (£££)

Another gastronomic temple, this time in one of Munich's top hotels, offering tempting regional delicacies as well as an extensive wine list in an elegant setting overlooking Karlsplatz.
⊞ N23 ⊠ Karlsplatz 25 ☎ 55 1 360 🕐 Lunch and dinner 🚇 U- or S-Bahn Karlsplatz

TANTRIS (£££)

The outside of the building is not very pretty, but inside you will find one of Munich's best restaurant. Managed by top chef Hans Haas, it offers a combination of international world-class service and cuisine.
⊞ K24 ⊠ Johann-Fichte-Strasse 7 ☎ 36 20 61 🕐 Tue–Sat lunch and dinner 🚇 U-Bahn Dietlindenstrasse

BAVARIAN RESTAURANTS

AUGUSTINER GROSSGASTSTÄTTEN (££)

Beer was brewed here in Munich's oldest still-standing brewery until 1897. This popular inn serves reasonably priced, traditional Bavarian fare in an authentic Munich atmosphere.

🚇 N23 ✉ Neuhauser Strasse 27 ☎ 551 99 257 🚇 U- or S-Bahn Karlsplatz

GEORGENHOF (££)

Enjoy game specialities and delicious apple strudel in this cosy, rustic restaurant, lit by candles and an open fire.

🚇 L24 ✉ Friedrichstrasse 1 ☎ 39 31 01 🚇 U-Bahn Giselastrasse

HAXNBAUER (££)

Watch the cooks turning giant shanks of pork (*Schweinshax'n*) over open beechwood fires in this ancient inn. Huge, hearty portions for meat lovers.

🚇 N24 ✉ Münzstrasse 5 ☎ 29 16 21 00 🚇 U- or S-Bahn Marienplatz

HUNDSKUGEL (££)

Wind the clock back to the Middle Ages at Munich's oldest inn (1440).

🚇 N23 ✉ Hotterstrasse 18 ☎ 26 42 72 🚇 U- or S-Bahn Marienplatz

ISARBRÄU (££)

This converted railway station brews its own *Weissbier* and offers an unusual menu including *Lokomotiven Pfiff* and *Weissbiercreme*.

🚇 Off map to south ✉ Kreuzeckstrasse 2 ☎ 79 89 61 🚇 S-Bahn Grosshesselohe

NÜRNBERGER BRATWURSTGLÖCKL (£)

An ancient tavern, best known for its Nürnberger Bratwurst (sausages from Nuremberg), grilled over an open beechwood fire and served on a bed of sauerkraut.

🚇 N23 ✉ Frauenplatz 9 ☎ 22 03 85 🚇 U- or S-Bahn Marienplatz

RATSKELLER (££)

Good, solid cuisine under the vaulted arches of the New Town Hall's cellar.

🚇 N23 ✉ Marienplatz 8 ☎ 22 03 13 🚇 U- or S-Bahn Marienplatz

SPATENHAUS (££)

Opposite the opera and popular with the after-theatre crowd. Pleasant atmosphere, good service and an excellent menu.

🚇 N24 ✉ Residenzstrasse 12 ☎ 290 70 60 🚇 U- or S-Bahn Marienplatz

WEISSES BRAUHAUS (£)

Easily the best *Weisswürste* in town here, accompanied by a wickedly strong, dark *Weissbier*.

🚇 N24 ✉ Tal 10 ☎ 29 98 75 🚇 U-or S-Bahn Marienplatz

ZUR SCHWAIGE (££)

Nourishing traditional fare in the south wing of Schloss Nymphenburg (▶ 24) or in the delightful shady garden.

🚇 L19 ✉ Schloss Nymphenburg ☎ 17 44 21 🚇 Tram 12, 17

Sausages

Sausages of every shape, size and colour are undoubtedly the hallmark of a Bavarian diet. The famous Munich *Weisswürste* (white veal sausages flecked with parsley) must be served in a tureen of hot water, peeled before eating and smothered in sweet mustard. Tradition has it that a white sausage mustn't hear the chimes of midday, so everyone crowds the restaurants at 11 to enjoy this local delicacy. *Guten Appetit*!

INTERNATIONAL CUISINE

Foreign influences

Since foreigners make up nearly a quarter of Munich's population, it is hardly surprising to find that many of the 6,000 restaurants in the city offer international cuisine. Only English food is missing, but nobody seems to mind. Generally speaking, eating out is not cheap, and you need to reserve a table in most restaurants.

AUSTERNKELLER (££)
Munich's best address for international seafood specialities.
♦ N24 ✉ Stollbergstrasse 11
☎ 29 87 87 ⊙ Tue–Sun, evenings only 🚋 Tram 19

BENJARONG (£££)
One of Germany's top 10 Thai restaurants, with prices to match, but worth every *pfennig*.
♦ N24 ✉ Falckenbergstrasse 7 ☎ 291 30 55 ⊙ Lunch and dinner 🚋 Tram 19

BISTRO TERRINE (£££)
Exquisite French cuisine in smart art-deco surroundings.
♦ M24 ✉ Amalienstrasse 89
☎ 28 17 80 ⊙ Tue–Fri lunch, Tue–Sat dinner 🚇 U-Bahn Universität

CAFÉ GLOCKENSPIEL (£££)
One of Munich's most romantic settings, directly opposite the city's famous Glockenspiel. Also a popular café and bar.
♦ N24 ✉ Marienplatz 28
☎ 26 42 56 🚇 U- or S-Bahn Marienplatz

CHAO PRAYA (££)
Book in advance for this popular restaurant to enjoy its extensive, authentic Thai menu.
♦ M21 ✉ Nymphenburger Strasse 128 ☎ 129 31 90
⊙ Lunch and dinner. Closed Sundays 🚇 U-Bahn Rotkreuzplatz

CHURRASCO (££)
For the best steak and salad in town; only a stone's throw from Marienplatz.
♦ N24 ✉ Tal 8 ☎ 29 46 61

⊙ 11.30AM–11.30PM 🚇 U- or S-Bahn Marienplatz

DAITOKAI (£££)
Watching your personal cook prepare your Japanese meal at your table is only half the fun. The other half is eating the mouth-watering results.
♦ L24 ✉ Kurfürstenstrasse 59
☎ 271 14 21 ⊙ Lunch and dinner. Closed Sun 🚋 Tram 27

GRISSINI (££)
An excellent Italian restaurant, decorated like an Italian palazzo.
♦ K25 ✉ Helmtrudenstrasse 11 ☎ 36 10 12 13 ⊙ Closed Sat lunch 🚇 U-Bahn Dietlindenstrasse

JO PEÑA'S (££)
This Mexican restaurant is always packed because of its delicious *fajitas*, *burritos* and *tequilas*.
♦ O24 ✉ Buttermelcherstrasse 17 ☎ 22 64 63 ⊙ Evenings only 🚋 Tram 18

KYTARO (££)
An atmospheric Greek restaurant guaranteeing a lively evening out.
♦ N25 ✉ Innere Wienerstrasse 36 ☎ 480 11 76
🚋 Tram 18

LA STELLA (££)
The young frequent this trattoria for its terrific pizzas.
♦ L24 ✉ Hohenstaufenstrasse 2 ☎ 34 17 79 🚇 U-Bahn Giselastrasse

LE CEZANNE (£££)
A tiny, original bistro specialising in Provençal dishes.
♦ L24 ✉ Konradstrasse 1

☎ 39 18 05 🕒 Evenings only
Ⓤ U-Bahn Giselastrasse

LE GAULOIS (££)
An ideal place to meet
Münchners. Try one of
the restaurant's famous
fondues.
✚ K24 ✉ Hörwarthstrasse 4
☎ 36 74 35 🕒 Evenings only.
Closed Sun 🚌 Bus 43, 44

MIFUNE (£££)
The owner of this classy
Japanese restaurant was
the star of the TV series
Shogun.
✚ M25 ✉ Ismaningerstrasse
136 ☎ 98 75 72 🚋 Tram 18

OSTERIA (£££)
Upmarket Italian
cuisine in beautiful
surroundings in this
historic restaurant.
✚ M23 ✉ Schellingstrasse 62
☎ 272 03 07 🕒 Closed Sun
🚌 Bus 53

PAPATAKIS (££)
The place to be at
weekends, if plate-
throwing and dancing
on the tables is your
scene.
✚ L24 ✉ Römerstrasse 15
☎ 34 13 05 🕒 Evenings only
🚌 Bus 33

**PRINCESS GARDEN
(££)**
Reputedly the best
Chinese restaurant in
town, directly opposite
the Hofbräuhaus.
✚ N24 ✉ Am Platzl 1a
☎ 34 38 37 Ⓤ U- or S-Bahn
Marienplatz

**RUE DES HALLES
(£££)**
Dine in a sophisticated,
Parisianatmosphere in
the fashionable
Haidhausen area.

✚ 025 ✉ Steinstrasse 18
☎ 48 56 75 🕒 Evenings only
Ⓢ S-Bahn Rosenheimer Platz

SEOUL (££)
Munich's only Korean
restaurant, located right in
the heart of Schwabing,
with delicious, albeit
unusual cuisine.
✚ K24 ✉ Leopoldstrasse 122
☎ 34 81 04 🕒 Lunch and
dinner Ⓤ U-Bahn Münchener
Freiheit

SHOYA (££)
Book early for this
authentic, realistically
priced Japanese
restaurant.
✚ M23 ✉ Gabelsbergerstrasse
85 ☎ 523 62 49 🕒 Evenings
only. Closed Sun Ⓤ U-Bahn
Theresienstrasse

TRADER VIC'S (£££)
A varied menu ranging
from Wanton soup to
barbecued spare ribs or
Calcutta lobster.
Excellent cocktails.
✚ N23 ✉ Hotel Bayerischer
Hof, Promenadeplatz 6 ☎ 22
61 92-94 🕒 Evenings only
(until 3AM) Ⓤ U- or S-Bahn
Marienplatz

TRZESNIEWSKI (££)
This 'in' brasserie,
opposite the Neue
Pinakothek, is packed
from breakfast until the
early hours.
✚ M23 ✉ Theresienstrasse 72
☎ 28 23 49 🚋 Tram 27

WERNECKHOF (£££)
Heavenly French fare
on a quiet backstreet
close to the English
Garden.
✚ L24 ✉ Werneckstrasse 11
☎ 39 99 36 🕒 Evenings only
Ⓤ U-Bahn Giselastrasse

'Mahlzeit!'

Mahlzeiten (mealtimes) are
comparatively early in Munich,
because most people start work
so early (around 7–8AM). Lunch
is eaten between 11:30 and 2
and is for many the main meal
of the day, followed by a light
supper or *Abendbrot* ('evening
bread'). Restaurants usually
serve dinner between 6:30 and
11PM when it is polite to wish
fellow diners *'Guten Appetit'*.
However, during the day it is
more common to hear the word
'Mahlzeit'.

BREAKFAST CAFÉS

Spoilt for choice

With such a thriving café scene, breakfast in Munich is very much a way of life. (There are even a couple of home-delivery breakfast services in town!) For a really unusual breakfast, visit Mangostin. Here you will find three restaurants (Japanese, Thai and Colonial style) combining to offer a sumptuous, exotic, all-you-can-eat breakfast with specialities from all over Asia. Even the beer garden serves spring rolls and saté!

CAFÉ EXTRABLATT
Breakfast – ranging from anything from *Weisswürste* to bacon and eggs – is served here until midnight.
🏠 L24 ✉ Leopoldstrasse 7 ☎ 33 33 33 Ⓤ U-Bahn Giselastrasse

CAFÉ HAIDHAUSEN
Look out for the 'Hangover' breakfast here, or try a romantic 'Romeo and Juliet' breakfast for two, served until 4PM.
🏠 025 ✉ Franziskanerstrasse 4 ☎ 688 60 43 Ⓢ S-Bahn Rosenheimer Platz

CAFÉ SCHWABING
Bavarian, French or Swiss-style breakfasts are the speciality of this trendy café. Excellent coffee too.
🏠 L23 ✉ Belgradstrasse 1 ☎ 308 88 56 🚋 Tram 12; bus 33

CAFÉ WIENER PLATZ
A chic crowd tends to frequent this modern coffee-house with its extensive breakfast menu.
🏠 N25 ✉ Innere-Wiener-Strasse 48 ☎ 448 94 94 🚋 Tram 19

GÜNTHER MURPHY'S
A popular Irish café specialising in all-you-can-eat Sunday brunches which are served all day long.
🏠 L24 ✉ Nikolaistrasse 9 ☎ 39 89 11 Ⓤ U-Bahn Giselastrasse

KAFFEEHAUS ALTSCHWABING
Enjoy a leisurely breakfast in this elegant café with tasteful *Jugendstil* décor.
🏠 M23 ✉ Schellingstrasse 56 ☎ 273 10 22 🚋 Tram 27; bus 53

MANGOSTIN
The huge Asian breakfast buffet served here on Sundays is a real treat (see panel).
🏠 R22 ✉ Maria-Einsiedl-Strasse 2 ☎ 723 20 31 🕐 Sundays only (from 11AM) Ⓤ U-Bahn Thalkirchen

MÖVENPICK
Munich's biggest breakfast; a 30m-long buffet table laden with sumptuous dishes, in a palatial ballroom. Reservation is essential.
🏠 N23 ✉ Lenbachplatz 8 ☎ 55 78 65 🕐 Sundays only Ⓤ U- or S-Bahn Karlsplatz

NEWS BAR
Catch up on the news over breakfast with a huge selection of international newspapers and magazines in this smart student meeting-place.
🏠 M24 ✉ Amalienstrasse 55 ☎ 28 17 87 Ⓤ U-Bahn Universität

ROXY'S
Great for people-watching, although. crowded and smoky. Very much an 'in' place to be seen.
🏠 L24 ✉ Leopoldstrasse 48 ☎ 34 92 92 Ⓤ U-Bahn Giselastrasse

TEA, COFFEE & ICE-CREAM CAFÉS

ADAMELLO

This Italian-run café sells the best ice-cream in town (see panel).

🕂 025 ☒ Preysingerstrasse 29 ☎ 48 32 83 🚋 Tram 18

ARZMILLER

A popular post-shopping haunt in a peaceful courtyard near Odeonsplatz.

🕂 N24 ☒ Salvatorstrasse 2, Theatinerhof ☎ 29 42 73 🕘 Shopping hours 🚇 U-Bahn Odeonsplatz

CAFÉ LUITPOLD PALMENGARTEN

Very smart and very expensive. Beside the ornamental fountain in a most exclusive shopping arcade.

🕂 N24 ☒ Brienner Strasse 11 ☎ 29 28 65 🕘 Weekdays 9–8; Sat 8–7 🚇 U-Bahn Odeonsplatz

CAFÉ MÜNCHENER FREIHEIT

One of Munich's top addresses for cakes and confectionery. Pleasant in summer.

🕂 L24 ☒ Münchener Freiheit 20 ☎ 34 90 80 🚇 U-Bahn Münchener Freiheit

CAFÉ PUCK

A spacious, trendy student haunt in the heart of Schwabing.

🕂 M24 ☒ Türkenstrasse 33 ☎ 280 22 80 🚇 U-Bahn Universität

HOTEL VIER JAHRESZEITEN

Enjoy a traditional English afternoon tea in one of the top hotels.

🕂 N24 ☒ Maximilianstrasse 17 ☎ 21 25 0 🕘 From 3PM 🚋 Tram 19

MÖVENPICK

One of the city's classic coffee-houses. The ice-cream is also hard to beat for quality and quantity, with scoops the size of tennis balls.

🕂 N23 ☒ Lenbachplatz 8 ☎ 55 78 65 🚇 U- or S-Bahn Karlsplatz

SARCLETTIS EIS-ECKE

The largest ice-cream menu in town, with over 100 flavours.

🕂 M21 ☒ Nymphenburger Strasse 155 ☎ 15 53 14 🚇 U-Bahn Rotkreuzplatz

SCHLOSS CAFÉ DACHAU

The very best gateaux in Munich in a magnificent palace setting.

🕂 Off map to northwest ☒ Schloss Dachau ☎ (08131) 874 75 🕘 11–6 🚇 S-Bahn Dachau

SCHLOSSCAFÉ PALMENHAUS

An elegant café in the Nymphenburg Palace's giant palm house.

🕂 L19 ☒ Schloss Nymphenburg ☎ 17 53 09 🕘 10–6 🚋 Tram 12, 17

VENEZIA

The best of many ice-cream cafés on Leopoldstrasse.

🕂 L24 ☒ Leopoldstrasse 31 ☎ 39 55 40 🚇 U-Bahn Giselastrasse

Ice-cream experts

Hidden in a quiet backstreet in Haidhausen, Adamello is a real find for any ice-cream addict. Recently described as selling the best ice-cream between here and Hamburg, Adamello (named after a mountain in the Dolomites) has an intimate chalet atmosphere. The speciality – *Coppa Adamello* – containing a mountain liqueur, is quite delicious, as is the lemon and champagne sorbet.

WHERE TO EAT

VEGETARIAN RESTAURANTS

Vegetarian surprise

Think of Bavarian cuisine and many people conjure up images of enormous joints of meat and miles of sausages. However, Munich offers some excellent vegetarian restaurants. Their menus are particularly interesting during *Spargelzeit* (Asparagus Season) in May and June when you will be amazed at the huge variety of ways in which to serve asparagus.

BALTZER (££)
Restaurant specialising in appetising vegetarian strudels.
✚ L21 ✉ Volkartstrasse 70 ☎ 12 39 19 19 🕐 Tue–Sat 6AM–10:30PM 🚇 U-Bahn Rotkreuzplatz

BUXS (£)
Pay by the weight of the plate in this cafeteria-style restaurant which provides an impressive array of hot and cold dishes.
✚ N24 ✉ Frauenstrasse 9 ☎ 29 36 84 🕐 Mon–Fri 11–8; Sat 9–3; Thu until 9PM 🚇 S-Bahn Isartor

CAFÉ IGNAZ (£)
One of Munich's few non-smoking cafés, with the added bonus of serving some of the best vegetarian pizzas and risotto in town.
✚ L23 ✉ Georgenstrasse 67 ☎ 271 60 93 🕐 Mon–Fri 7AM–10PM, Sat from 9AM 🚇 U-Bahn Josephsplatz

CAFÉ RUFFINI (£)
Offers an outstanding organic vegetarian menu, together with equally good occasional meat dishes.
✚ L21 ✉ Orffstrasse 22 ☎ 16 11 60 🕐 Tue–Sat 10AM–midnight; Sun 10–6 🚇 U-Bahn Rotkreuzplatz

DAS GOLLIER (£)
Serves enterprising dishes in a casual, arty atmosphere. Live music is often performed at night.
✚ N21 ✉ Gollierstrasse 83 ☎ 50 16 73 🕐 Daily 5PM–midnight, lunch weekdays only 🚇 U-Bahn Heimeranplatz

GOURMET'S GARDEN (£)
A small vegetarian delicatessen in Schwabing.
✚ L23 ✉ Belgradstrasse 9 ☎ 308 84 93 🕐 Weekdays 9:30–7:30; Thu until 8 🚋 Tram 12, 27; bus 33

LOBEWEINS (£)
A tiny, simple bistro with a daily changing menu, superb soups and tempting cakes.
✚ M24 ✉ Türkenstrasse 63 ☎ 271 27 67 🕐 Lunch only 🚇 U-Bahn Universität

PRINZ MYSHKIN (££)
This popular, trendy café offers a lengthy menu of creative dishes.
✚ N23 ✉ Hackenstrasse 2 ☎ 26 55 96 🕐 Daily 11AM–midnight 🚇 U- or S-Bahn Marienplatz

TOFU (£)
A Vietnamese vegetarian café.
✚ N24 ✉ Herrnstrasse 11 ☎ 290 41 35 🕐 Weekdays 11–3, 5–11; Sat noon–11 🚇 S-Bahn Isartor

SNACKS

CASA DELFIN (£)

Popular with *tapas* fans.

🕂 L23 ✉ Elisabethmarkt
☎ 2 71 02 01 🕑 Weekdays
10–6; Sat 8–1 🚋 Tram 27

CROQUE LADEN (£)

Giant, warm, crusty baguettes with delicious fillings.

🕂 Off map to north
✉ Milbertshofener Strasse 43
☎ 35 24 23 🕑 Weekdays
11–10 🚇 U-Bahn Frankfurter Ring

EDGAR'S MÜSLI-ECK (£)

Edgar's *Bircher-müsli* (yoghurt, fruit and muesli mixtures) are both filling and healthy.

🕂 N24 ✉ Viktualienmarkt
🕑 Shop hours 🚇 U- or S-Bahn Marienplatz

MÖVENPICK MARCHÉ (£)

The food is all freshly cooked in front of you at this unusual, self-service, indoor market.

🕂 N23 ✉ Neuhauser Strasse 19 ☎ 26 06 06 1 🚇 U- or S-Bahn Marienplatz

MÜNCHNER SUPPENKÜCHE (£)

Try the *Pfannekuchensuppe* (pancake soup) or *Leberknödelsuppe* (liver dumpling soup) at this soup kitchen.

🕂 N24 ✉ Viktualienmarkt
🕑 Shop hours 🚇 U- or S-Bahn Marienplatz

NORDSEE (£)

This fishmonger offers a range of hot and cold dishes. Standing room only.

🕂 N24 ✉ Viktualienmarkt
☎ 22 11 86 🕑 Mon–Fri 8–6
🚇 U- or S-Bahn Marienplatz

STRUDELSTUBE (£)

A take-away strudel shop. The *Topfenstrudel* is particularly tasty.

🕂 N24 ✉ Orlandostrasse 4
☎ 29 85 87 🕑 10–10
🚇 U- or S-Bahn Marienplatz

TIRAMISU (£)

This tiny Italian bar serves excellent *antipasti* and has a daily changing pasta menu.

🕂 L23 ✉ Hohenzollernstrasse 124 ☎ 308 60 08
🕑 Weekdays 11.30–10
🚇 U-Bahn Hohenzollernplatz

VINCENZ MURR (£)

Help yourself at the extensive salad bar, then have a picnic by the fountain opposite, at Rindermarkt.

🕂 N23 ✉ Rosenstrasse 7
☎ 260 47 65 🕑 Shop hours
🚇 U- or S-Bahn Marienplatz

VINI E PANINI (£)

Not only bread and wine but also delicious snacks from different regions of Italy.

🕂 L24 ✉ Nordendstrasse 45
☎ 2 72 17 43 🕑 Shop hours
🚋 Tram 27

WOKMAN (£)

Cheap Chinese fast food.

🕂 L24 ✉ Leopoldstrasse 68
☎ 39 03 43 🚇 U-Bahn Münchener Freiheit

Bavarian fare

Any excuse is found for a quick snack or *Brotzeit* ('bread time') in Munich, to tide you over until the serious eating begins. The city's countless snack-bars (usually called *Kneipe*, *Lokal* or *Schnellimbiss*) and butchers' shops (*Metzgereien*) often serve such specialities as *Leberkäs* (a meatloaf of beef, pork and spices), *Kartoffelpuffer* (potato fritters), *Radi* (thin slices of salted horseradish) and, of course, sausages.

SHOPPING AREAS

Bargain-hunting

There are plenty of bargains to be had if you know where to look. Start with the department stores which sell cut-price goods in their basements, and always keep your eyes open for *Sonderangebot* (special offer) signs. As always, the best bargains can be found at the end of season sales in January and July, often with astonishing discounts.

Opening times

Most shops are usually open weekdays from 9 until 6:30, with late-night shopping (*Stadtabend*) on Thursdays until 8:30. Don't leave it until Saturday to buy your presents as most shops close at 1 or 2PM, apart from the first Saturday in every month when they remain open until 4. Legislation now permits shops to stay open until 8 on weekdays, until 4 on Saturdays, so opening times may change.

Munich has over 8,000 shops and 15 big department stores catering for all tastes and pockets.

ANTIQUES

All over Schwabing there are shops specialising in antiques, in particular 'English', Jugendstil (art nouveau), or art deco. Hunt in the narrow alleys off Tal and behind the Viktualienmarkt for bargains or visit one of the many auction houses dotted about town.

ARTS & CRAFTS

Browse through Maximilianstrasse's 25 galleries or explore Briennerstrasse, Theatinerstrasse and the arcades of the Hofgarten. For the finest in Bavarian handicrafts, visit the Kunstgewerbe-Verein in Pacellistrasse or look in the numerous streets converging on Max-Joseph-Platz.

BOOKSHOPS

There are a staggering 300 publishing houses in Munich and a wide variety of bookshops concentrated in the city centre and near the university in Schellingstrasse.

FASHION

You will be amazed at the range of boutiques from *haute couture* to Bavarian folk costume and the most unusual new trends. In the elegant, smart shops of Theatinerstrasse, Residenzstrasse and Maximilianstrasse you

will find famous names such as Yves Saint Laurent, Armani and Hermès. Even the small side-roads, with their mazes of attractive arcades and passages leading to Residenz-strasse, are packed with chic designer boutiques.

The most popular shopping street is the pedestrian zone between Karlsplatz and Marienplatz, where huge department stores are interspersed with elegant boutiques and everyday shops. In summer you will find buskers and street entertainers every few metres.

The smart shops of Sendlingerstrasse bridge the price gap between the exclusive Maximilianstrasse area and the pedestrian zone, with smart fashions, imaginative gift shops and giant sports and department stores. Head to the lively shopping area of Schwabing for creative and stylish clothes to suit every purse. Near the university you are sure to find something really original in the way-out shops and second-hand stores.

INTERIOR DESIGN

Check out Ludwigstrasse, Briennerstrasse and Tal for quality furnishings and designer gadgets.

JEWELLERY

Maximilianstrasse has many famous jewellers including Bulgari, while there are some more reasonably priced shops in Schwabing.

GIFTS & BAVARIAN SOUVENIRS

ETCETERA
Full of novel Bavarian souvenirs and things you would love to buy but don't really need.
➕ N24 ✉ Wurzerstrasse 12 ☎ 22 60 68 🚇 U- or S-Bahn Marienplatz

GESCHENKE KAISER
Pewter Christmas decorations, serving dishes, candlesticks and beer jugs are the specialities here.
➕ N24 ✉ Rindermarkt 1 ☎ 26 45 09 🚇 U- or S-Bahn Marienplatz

I-DÜPFERL
Three floors of tempting ideas for holiday gifts, including fun household gadgets and knick-knacks.
➕ N23 ✉ Sendlinger Strasse 37 ☎ 260 50 48 🚇 U-Bahn Sendlinger Tor

KUNSTGEWERBE-VEREIN
Shop here for high-quality, carved, painted and handcrafted Bavarian products from puppets and pottery to jewellery and carnival masks – truly exclusive gifts.
➕ N23 ✉ Pacellistrasse 6–8 ☎ 290 14 70 🚇 U- or S-Bahn Karlsplatz

LEDERHOSEN WAGNER
This shop has been making leather shorts from soft deer-skin since 1825. Surprise your friends with a 'shaving brush' hat, made out of chamois hair, to match the shorts.
➕ M24 ✉ Tal 2 ☎ 22 56 97 🚇 U- or S-Bahn Marienplatz

LODEN FREY
Chose your *Trachten* (folk costume) at the largest specialist store for national costume in the world. Children love the toboggan run from the ground floor to the basement (see panel).
➕ N23 ✉ Maffeistrasse 7–9 ☎ 23 69 30 🚇 U- or S-Bahn Marienplatz

MÜNCHNER GESCHENKE-STUBEN
This shop is crammed with every imaginable Bavarian souvenir.
➕ N24 ✉ Petersplatz 8 ☎ 26 74 56 🚇 U- or S-Bahn Marienplatz

MÜNCHNER MUSIKDOSEN
The traditional musical boxes here make a perfect gift to take home.
➕ N24 ✉ Pfisterstrasse 8 ☎ 290 40 91 🚇 U- or S-Bahn Marienplatz

STOCKHAMMER
Idea-hungry shoppers are sure to find original gifts here.
➕ L24 ✉ Hohenzollernstrasse 33 ☎ 34 77 81 🚇 U- or S-Bahn Münchener Freiheit

WALLACH
This famous rococo-fronted shop is full of Bavarian atmosphere and attractive gifts, including fantastic hand-printed fabrics and *Dirndls* (see panel).
➕ N24 ✉ Residenzstrasse 3 ☎ 22 08 71 🚇 U- or S-Bahn Marienplatz

Traditional *Trachten*

The nice thing about *Trachten* (Bavarian national costume) is that Münchners really do wear it, especially on Sundays, holidays or festive occasions. Most popular are the *Lederhosen* and the smart green-collared grey jackets for men or the gaily-coloured *Dirndl* dresses with fitted bodices and full gathered skirts. You will enjoy wandering around Loden Frey, Munich's top outlet for such outfits, where there is a never-ending choice of styles.

DEPARTMENT STORES, FOOD STORES & MARKETS

Ludwig Beck

Beck is without doubt Munich's smartest department store, known for its ever-changing décor created by well-known artists. Its departments range from lingerie to CDs and from designer clothing to gifts. At Christmas, the shop is transformed into a winter wonderland of handicrafts with artisans at work on the top floor. Round off your visit to this Munich institution with a snack at the oriental Sum Bar.

BOETTNER
One of Munich's oldest hostelries, well known for schnapps, caviare and other delicacies.
N24 ⊠ Theatinerstrasse 8 ☎ 22 12 10 U- or S-Bahn Marienplatz

DALLMAYR
The city's top delicatessen, which used to supply the Bavarian royal family. The first floor serves a heavenly champagne breakfast.
N24 ⊠ Dienerstrasse 14-15 ☎ 213 51 00 U- or S-Bahn Marienplatz

EILLES
One of several Eilles stores, selling some of the finest tea, coffee and wines.
N24 ⊠ Residenzstrasse 13 ☎ 22 61 84 U- or S-Bahn Marienplatz

ELISABETHMARKT
Schwabing's answer to the Viktualienmarkt, with surprisingly few tourists.
L23 ⊠ Elisabethplatz 🚋 Tram 27

ELLY SEIDL
A tiny chocolate shop, famous for its morish pralines and its '*Münchner Kuppeln*' (chocolates resembling the onion-domes of the Frauenkirche).
N24 ⊠ Am Kosttor 2 ☎ 22 15 22 U- or S-Bahn Marienplatz

HERTIE
This branch of the Hertie department store chain stretches from the main station to Karlsplatz and offers everyday items at reasonable prices.
N23 ⊠ Bahnhofplatz ☎ 551 20 U- or S-Bahn Hauptbahnhof

KÄFER
An epicurean labyrinth selling food and drink from around the world in the smart Bogenhausen district.
N25 ⊠ Prinzregentenstrasse 73 ☎ 416 81 U-Bahn Prinzregentenplatz

KARSTADT
This giant department store is divided into three: Haus Oberpollinger am Dom sells goods like electical appliances, books and furnishings; Karstadt am Karlstor offers cosmetics and clothing; Karstadt Sporthaus Oberpollinger stocks sports items.
N23 ⊠ Neuhauser Strasse 18 ☎ 29 02 30 U- or S-Bahn Karlsplatz

KAUFHOF
One of several Kaufhof department stores in Munich, recently refurbished and in a central position.
N24 ⊠ Kaufingerstrasse 2 ☎ 23 18 51 U- or S-Bahn Marienplatz

LA MAISON DU VIN
There is an exceptional range of fine French wines here.
L24 ⊠ Nordendstrasse 62 ☎ 272 05 52 🚋 Tram 27

LE CHALET DU FROMAGE
One of the best

cheesemongers in Munich.

➕ L24 ✉ Stand 11, Elisabethplatz ☎ 271 22 43 🕐 Closed Mon 🚊 Tram 27

LUDWIG BECK

A Munich landmark and, without doubt, one of the city's best stores (see panel opposite).

➕ N24 ✉ Marienplatz 11 ☎ 23 69 10 Ⓤ U- or S-Bahn Marienplatz

MARKT AM WIENER PLATZ

Tiny green wooden huts huddle round the maypole in Haidhausen, providing an attractive alternative to supermarket shopping.

➕ N25 ✉ Wiener Platz Ⓤ U-Bahn Max-Weber-Platz

OLYMPIA EINKAUFSZENTRUM (OEZ)

For everything under one roof, visit this massive shopping centre with over 100 shops near the Olympiapark.

➕ H21 ✉ Hanauerstrasse 68 ☎ 141 60 02 🚌 Bus 36

RISCHART

One of many Rischart shops offering the largest choice of bread, rolls and cakes in town.

➕ N24 ✉ Marienplatz 18 ☎ 231 70 00 Ⓤ U- or S-Bahn Marienplatz

SCHMIDT

Shop here for delicious *Lebkuchen* (gingerbread), presented in collectable tins, along with *Stollen* (fruitcakes) and cookies.

➕ N24 ✉ Westenriederstrasse 8a ☎ 29 50 68 Ⓢ S-Bahn Isartor

SPANISCHES

FRUCHTHAUS

The mouthwatering display of dried fruits entices you into this small shop with its unusual selection of crystallised, fresh and chocolate-coated fruits.

➕ N23 ✉ Rindermarkt 10 ☎ 26 45 70 Ⓤ U- or S-Bahn Marienplatz

SPORT-SCHECK

The department shop for sports fanatics; six floors dedicated to every sport imaginable. You can even arrange sporting activities or a cheap skiing day-trip on the sixth floor.

➕ N23 ✉ Sendlinger Strasse 85 ☎ 21 66 12 54 Ⓤ U-Bahn Sendlinger Tor

THE BRITISH SHOP

Baked beans, pasties, tomato ketchup, even Christmas pudding for the homesick!

➕ M23 ✉ Schellingstrasse 100 ☎ 52 25 04 🚌 Bus 53

VIKTUALIENMARKT

The largest and most famous Bavarian open-air food market, near the bustling city centre.

➕ N24 Ⓤ U- or S-Bahn Marienplatz

ZERWIRKGEWÖLBE

This unique butchers' shop, specialising in game, is the oldest of its kind in Germany, dating from the 18th century. It also serves tasty snacks.

➕ N23 ✉ Ledererstrasse 3 ☎ 22 68 24 Ⓤ U- or S-Bahn Marienplatz

Flea markets

Flea markets have long been a tradition in Munich, offering fun shopping either in the small impromptu markets or in the large, well-organised, commercial ones in Arnulfstrasse or in the grounds of the Pfanni factory on the east side of Munich. One of Munich's largest and most popular market takes place on the first day of the *Frühlingsfest* (Spring Festival) in April.

73

SPECIALIST SHOPS

CARDIAC DESIGNHAUS

The emphasis here is on fun designer gifts and household goods.
⊞ N24　⊠ Tal 20　☎ 29 78 08　ⓊU- or S-Bahn Marienplatz

DAS LANDHAUSECK

An amazing cornucopia of traditional Bavarian furniture and antiques.
⊞ N23　⊠ St Jacobs-Platz 12　☎ 260 95 72　ⓊU-Bahn Sendlinger Tor

DEHNER

Full of great gift ideas for garden lovers. What about a packet of Alpine flower seeds or even a grow-your-own 'Bavarian meadow' lawn?
⊞ N24　⊠ Frauenstrasse 8　☎ 291 38 88　Ⓢ S-Bahn Isartor

DIE PUPPENSTUBE

The dolls and puppets here will take you back to your childhood.
⊞ M23　⊠ Luisenstrasse 68　☎ 272 32 67　🚌 Bus 53

FOURTH DIMENSION

One of Germany's leading costume jewellery shops. Smart but affordable.
⊞ L23　⊠ Herzogstrasse 79　☎ 307 20 23　ⓊU-Bahn Hohenzollernstrasse

GALLERY M

Everything imaginable for a trendy home in this chic, modern interior design shop.
⊞ M23　⊠ Schleissheimer Strasse 6　☎ 52 56 18　ⓊU-Bahn Stiglmaiersplatz

HEMMERLE

The treasures in this traditional Munich jeweller's are expensive but very solid.
⊞ N24　⊠ Maximilianstrasse 14　☎ 22 53 30　🚋 Tram 19

HIEBER AM DOM

One of the best places for CDs, tapes and sheet music.
⊞ N23　⊠ Liebfrauenstrasse 1　☎ 29 00 80 14　ⓊU- or S-Bahn Marienplatz

HUGENDUBEL

Bookworms love this giant book 'supermarket', spread over four floors in one of several branches dotted throughout Munich. There are even settees where you can sit and read without buying.
⊞ N24　⊠ Marienplatz　☎ 23 89 0　ⓊU- or S-Bahn Marienplatz

KUNST UND SPIEL

A magical shop full of sturdy, educational toys together with an extensive arts and craft section.
⊞ L24　⊠ Leopoldstrasse 48　☎ 381 62 70　ⓊU-Bahn Giselastrasse

LANDPARTIE

A cosy country atmosphere welcomes you into this homely shop, crammed with both antique furniture and household accessories.
⊞ L24　⊠ Kurfürstenstrasse 12　☎ 34 85 98　🚋 Tram 27

LEUTE – ALLES AUS HOLZ

Everything here is made of wood, with decorative and functional items from games to biscuit forms.

Museum pieces

Still struggling to find a really original present to take home for friends and relatives? Then head for the Deutsches Museum shop (Museumsladen Deutsches Museum) for the most amazing and eccentric variety of books, toys, puzzles and models based on the scientific and technical world, catering for children and adults alike.

✠ N24 ✉ Viktualienmarkt 2 ☎ 26 82 48 🚇 U- or S-Bahn Marienplatz

NEIDHARDT
This fine antique store specialises in 18th-century furniture.
✠ N24 ✉ Briennerstrasse 11 ☎ 22 06 19 🚇 U-Bahn Odeonsplatz

NEWS AND MORE
Germany's first media store has a vast range of electronic literature, software and computer games, offering shoppers the chance to cruise the Internet.
✠ N24 ✉ Sendlinger Strasse 28 ☎ 26 02 26 80 🚇 U-Bahn Sendlinger Tor

NYMPHENBURGER PORZELLANMANU–FAKTUR
This famous porcelain manufacturer still turns out traditional rococo designs. Based in Nymphenburg Palace, with this outlet in the town centre.
✠ N24 ✉ Odeonsplatz 1 ☎ 28 24 28 🕐 Closed Sat 🚇 U-Bahn Odeonsplatz

PERLENMARKT
A unique store selling nothing but buttons, beads and jewellery-making equipment.
✠ L24 ✉ Nordendstrasse 28 ☎ 271 05 76 🚋 Tram 27

RAHMEN-MAYR
You will always remember your visit if you take home a print, etching or original painting of the city from here.

✠ O24 ✉ Reichenbachstrasse 26 ☎ 201 45 63 🚇 U-Bahn Fraunhoferstrasse

SCHWABINGER TRÖDELMARKT
The city's most attractive collection of antique and junk shops of all styles and genres. Great on a rainy day.
✠ J25 ✉ Neusser Strasse 21 ☎ 36 01 04 79 🕐 Fri and Sat only 🚇 U-Bahn Alte Heide

SEIDL
An Aladdin's cave of antique porcelain, silver, jewellery, dolls and paintings.
✠ L24 ✉ Siegesstrasse 21 ☎ 34 95 68 🕐 Closed Sat 🚇 U-Bahn Münchener Freiheit

SPIELWAREN SCHMIDT
One of the big names in toys, with Steiff bears and cuddly animals a speciality.
✠ N23 ✉ Neuhauser Strasse 31 ☎ 231 86 02 🚇 U- or S-Bahn Karlsplatz

STEIGERWALD
The top address for porcelain, silver and glass.
✠ N24 ✉ Amiraplatz 1 ☎ 22 42 00 🚇 U-Bahn Odeonsplatz

WORDS WORTH
Situated in a picturesque backyard, there is a large range of English books, a Pooh Corner for children and even a small National Trust shop.
✠ M24 ✉ Schellingstrasse 21a ☎ 280 91 41 🚌 Bus 53

Toys
Germany has been one of the world's leading toy manufacturers since the Middle Ages, particularly famous for its china dolls, tin plate toys and Steiff teddy bears, with many important manufacturing centres based around Munich including Nuremberg, Oberammergau and Berchtesgaden. Today old Steiff bears are considered great collector's pieces, with the record going to one called 'Teddy Girl' which was sold for £110,000 at auction in December 1994.

FASHION SHOPS

Rudolph Moshammer

It would be hard to find a more eccentric Münchner in the world of fashion than flamboyant couturier Rudolph Moshammer. He is easy to spot around town in his gleaming white Rolls Royce with Daisy, his little Yorkshire terrier. His boutique on the magnificent Maximilianstrasse has become a Munich attraction with masterpieces in silk, velvet and satin. Devotees include princes and sheikhs, even Arnold Schwarzenegger.

BOGNER

This classic Munich company sells everything from sports clothes to traditional costume for both men and women.
🕂 N24 ✉ Residenzstrasse 15 ☎ 290 70 40 🚇 U- or S-Bahn Marienplatz

BREE

Smart suitcases, handbags, wallets, belts and more.
🕂 N24 ✉ Theatinerhof, Salvatorstrasse 2 ☎ 29 87 45 🚇 U-Bahn Odeonsplatz

EDUARD MEIER

Munich's oldest shoe shop (famous since 1596) with leather sofas and first-class service.
🕂 N24 ✉ Residenzstrasse 22 ☎ 22 00 44 🚇 U- or S-Bahn Marienplatz

HALLHUBER

Popular with young shoppers – leading labels at reasonable prices.
🕂 L24 ✉ Leopoldstrasse 25 ☎ 38 30 81 10 🚇 U-Bahn Münchener Freiheit

HIRMER

Six floors exclusively for men at this first-class clothing store.
🕂 N23 ✉ Kaufingerstrasse 22 ☎ 23 68 30 🚇 U- or S-Bahn Marienplatz

KONEN

A reliable fashion store full of leading international labels.
🕂 N23 ✉ Sendlingerstrasse 3 ☎ 23 50 20 🚇 U-Bahn Sendlinger Tor

MCM

This world-famous accessory store has its flagship here in Munich.
🕂 N24 ✉ Residenzstrasse 19–20 ☎ 29 03 90 00 🚇 U- or S-Bahn Marienplatz

OILILY

Brightly coloured, patterned casual clothes for children. The floral wellies are especially fun.
🕂 L24 ✉ Hohenzollernstrasse 43 ☎ 334 96 37 🚇 U-Bahn Münchener Freiheit

PATAGONIA

The only Patagonia store in Germany, selling stylish but practical sports clothing.
🕂 L24 ✉ Leopoldstrasse 47 ☎ 39 92 99 🚇 U-Bahn Münchener Freiheit

RUDOLF MOSHAMMER

Munich's most famous tailor (see panel).
🕂 N24 ✉ Maximilianstrasse 14 ☎ 22 69 24 🚋 Tram 19

SCHLICHTING

A vast choice of fashion items for children, teens and mothers-to-be, along with toys and games.
🕂 N24 ✉ Weinstrasse 8 ☎ 29 49 47 🚇 U- or S-Bahn Marienplatz

THERESA

Trendy and out-rageously expensive designer fashions, mainly Italian prêt-à-porter.
🕂 N24 ✉ Theatinerstrasse 31 ☎ 22 48 45 🚇 U-Bahn Odeonsplatz

CINEMAS & NIGHTCLUBS

CINEMAS

CINEMA
Probably the best cinema in town, with four different films daily, mostly undubbed.
✚ M22 ✉ Nymphenburger Strasse 31 ☎ 55 52 55 Ⓜ U-Bahn Stiglmaierplatz

IMAX
Germany's first state-of-the-art IMAX cinema shows fascinating nature films on one of Europe's biggest screens.
✚ 024 ✉ Forum der Technik ☎ 21 12 51 80 Ⓢ S-Bahn Isartor

MUSEUM LICHTSPIELE
This former music-hall frequently shows English-language films.
✚ 024 ✉ Lilienstrasse 2 ☎ 48 24 03 🚌 Bus 52,56

NEUES ARRI
One of Munich's main 'art film' cinemas. Every November a competition for European Film Colleges is held here.
✚ M24 ✉ Türkenstrasse 91 ☎ 38 19 04 50 Ⓜ U-Bahn Universität

NIGHTCLUBS

NACHTWERK
This former warehouse offers plenty of space for dancing and is increasingly becoming a popular venue for live bands.
✚ N20 ✉ Landsbergerstrasse 185 ☎ 578 38 00 🕐 10:30PM–4AM Ⓢ S-Bahn Donnersbergerbrücke 🚊 Tram 18, 19

P1
An extremely chic club in the basement of the Haus der Kunst with eight different bars frequented by models, jet-setters and celebrities.
✚ M24 ✉ Prinzregentenstrasse 1 ☎ 29 42 52 🕐 10PM–4AM Ⓜ U-Bahn Lehel

PARK CAFÉ
This enormous club has long been a favourite, with music for all tastes in an unlikely rococo setting.
✚ N23 ✉ Sophienstrasse 7 ☎ 59 83 13 🕐 Tue–Thu 10PM–3AM; Fri and Sat until 7AM Ⓜ U-Bahn Königsplatz

PFANNI FACTORY
In this old factory, Wolfgang Nöth, the Munich mogul who specialises in large barn-like venues, continues the party tradition of the old Riem airport, now given over to a new trade fair centre.
✚ P26 ✉ Grossinger Strasse 6 Ⓜ U- or S-Bahn Ostenhof

SKYLINE
Dance at this New York-style bar and dance club high above the roofs of Schwabing, while admiring the breathtaking views over Leopoldstrasse.
✚ L24 ✉ Leopoldstrasse 82 ☎ 33 31 31 🕐 8PM–4AM Ⓜ U-Bahn Münchener Freiheit

Cinemas galore
It is hardly surprising that Munich is a city of cinema-goers, with the Bavaria Film Studios, 83 cinemas and a series of film festivals, including a Documentary Film Festival in April, the major *Münchner Filmfest* in Gasteig in June, a Fantasy Film Festival in July and International Art Film Week in August. The European Film Colleges Festival rounds off the year in November.

BARS, CAFÉS & LIVE MUSIC

All-night partying

Compared with other major European cities, Munich's nightlife is relatively small-scale and provincial, due to early closing laws which prevent many places staying open all night. Nevertheless, if you know where to go, you can party till the early hours. Many bars close around 1AM and most nightclubs at 4AM. However, the Backstage Club, nicknamed 'House of the Rising Sun', with its Techno- and House-music doesn't even *open* until 6AM.

ALLOTRIA
An old traditional jazz club.
M23 ☒ Oskar-von-Miller Ring 3 ☎ 28 58 58 ⊙ U-Bahn Odeonsplatz

CAFÉ FRISCHHUT
Early birds meet night owls for a coffee and *Schmalznudeln* (delicious deep-fried pastries) at 5 in the morning here at the Viktualienmarkt.
N24 ☒ Prälat-Zistl-Strasse 8 ☎ 26 82 37 ⊙ Mon–Fri 5AM–5PM; Sat 5AM–1PM ⊙ U- or S-Bahn Marienplatz

CAFÉ GLOCKENSPIEL
Situated opposite Marienplatz's famous Glockenspiel, the roof-terrace cocktail bar, plush baroque-style bar and '70s-style Expresso bar-café here are always crowded.
N24 ☒ Marienplatz 28 (5th floor) ☎ 26 42 56 ⊙ Until 10AM–1AM ⊙ U- or S-Bahn Marienplatz

CAFÉ NEUHAUSEN
Mingle with the in-crowd at this stylish café with its long list of long drinks.
M21 ☒ Blutenbergstrasse 106 ☎ 123 62 88 ⊙ Daily 10AM–1AM ⊙ U-Bahn Rotkreuzplatz

HAUS DER 111 BIERE
The name 'House of 111 Beers' speaks for itself.
L24 ☒ Franzstrasse 3 ☎ 33 12 48 ⊙ Until midnight ⊙ U-Bahn Münchener Freiheit

HAVANNA CLUB
Ernest Hemingway used to drink in this dark, intimate bar decorated in true Spanish colonial style.
N24 ☒ Herrnstrasse 30 ☎ 29 18 84 ⊙ Mon–Thu 6–1; Fri 6–2; Sat 7–2; Sun 7–1 ⊙ S-Bahn Isartor

INTERVIEW
A stylish crowd frequents this modern American bar from early morning till late at night.
O24 ☒ Gärtnerplatz 1 ☎ 202 16 49 ⊙ 10–midnight, Sun until 7 ⊙ Bus 52, 56

IRISH FOLK PUB
One of many popular Irish bars. This one boasts 90 different malt whiskies, wholesome Irish food and live music on Thursdays.
L24 ☒ Giselastrasse 11 ☎ 34 24 46 ⊙ 8PM–1AM ⊙ U-Bahn Giselastrasse

JAZZCLUB UNTERFAHRT
One of the most important jazz clubs in Europe with modern jazz, bebop and avant-garde celebrities.
O26 ☒ Kirchenstrasse 96 ☎ 448 27 94 ⊙ Tue–Sun 8PM–1AM; Fri and Sat until 3AM ⊙ S-Bahn Ostbahnhof ⊙ Tram 19

JODLER WIRT
You would be forgiven for thinking you were in the heart of the Bavarian countryside in this tiny, folksy bar. Always crowded and jolly, often featuring local yodellers at night.
N24 ☒ Alterhofstrasse 4 ☎ 22 12 49 ⊙ Mon–Sat 6–1PM ⊙ U- or S-Bahn Marienplatz

JULEPS NEW YORK BAR

Spend happy hour here (5–8PM) with a choice of over 150 cocktails.

✚ 025 ✉ Breisacherstrasse 18 ☎ 448 00 44 🕐 Daily 7PM–1AM; Fri and Sat until 3AM Ⓢ S-Bahn Ostbahnhof

KAFFEE GIESING

Excellent live music, particularly jazz, blues and rock, and classical music for breakfast.

✚ Q23 ✉ Bergstrasse 5 ☎ 692 05 79 🕐 Mon–Sat 4PM–1AM; Sun 10AM–1PM Ⓤ U-Bahn Silberhornstrasse

MASTER'S HOME

A unique African colonial-style bar with a difference (see panel).

✚ N24 ✉ Frauenstrasse 11 ☎ 22 99 09 🕐 6PM–1AM; Fri and Sat until 3AM Ⓢ S-Bahn Isartor

NACHT CAFÉ

One of the most popular places for live music ranging from jazz and blues to flamenco, in a '50s-style bar.

✚ N23 ✉ Maximiliansplatz 5 ☎ 59 59 00 🕐 9PM–5AM Ⓤ U- or S-Bahn Karlsplatz

OKLAHOMA

Hurry on down to this authentic saloon bar with live country-and-western music.

✚ R22 ✉ Schäftlarnstrasse 156 ☎ 723 43 27 🕐 Wed–Sat 7–1AM Ⓤ U-Bahn Thalkirchen

SCHUMANN'S

It's hard to get a table here at Germany's number-one bar, but once inside you can enjoy watching Munich's '*Schickeria*' (chic set) at play, and spotting famous people, including one regular, Boris Becker.

✚ N24 ✉ Maximilianstrasse 36 ☎ 22 90 60 🕐 Daily except Sat 5PM–3AM 🚋 Tram 19

SCHWABINGER PODIUM

Enjoy a night of rock'n roll and blues in this small, popular venue.

✚ L24 ✉ Wagnerstrasse 1 ☎ 39 94 82 🕐 Daily 8PM–1PM Ⓤ U-Bahn Münchener Freiheit

WEINSTADL

The grand stone vaults of the oldest house in Munich provide a cosy venue for wine connoisseurs.

✚ N24 ✉ Burgstrasse 5 ☎ 22 10 47 🕐 Mon–Sat 10AM–midnight; Sun from 4PM Ⓤ U- or S-Bahn Marienplatz

WINCHESTER ARMS

An English pub in the heart of Schwabing, complete with ales, darts and pub food.

✚ 023 ✉ Maistrasse 53 ☎ 53 45 30 🕐 8PM–1AM Ⓤ U-Bahn Goetheplatz

WUNDERBAR

Come to this futuristic, cave-like bar with its fun crowd and chat to someone at a neighbouring table by Telekom at the weekly 'telephone parties'.

✚ N24 ✉ Hochbrückenstrasse 3 ☎ 29 51 18 🕐 8PM–3AM Ⓤ U- or S-Bahn Marienplatz

Out of Africa

Not only is Master's Home an extraordinary underground bar in the colonial style of a typical African farmhouse, but it also contains the furniture. You can choose whether to sit in the bathroom, the bedroom, the living room or at the bar, which is cooled by a giant aeroplane propeller, and eat, dance or simply lap up the atmosphere over a delicious albeit expensive cocktail.

THEATRE, CLASSICAL MUSIC, OPERA & BALLET

Musical Mecca

Munich and music go hand-in-hand. Its connection with Mozart, Wagner and Richard Strauss, not to mention its three symphony orchestras, has made it famous throughout the world. Today it plays host to major events in the musical calendar including the glamorous Opera Festival and the Summer Concert Season at Nymphenburg Palace. Try also to attend one of the summer open-air concerts at the Residenz, held in an atmospheric courtyard setting.

CUVILLIÉS-THEATER
Both opera and drama are popular at this magnificent theatre, venue for the première of Mozart's *Idomeneo*, and considered the finest rococo theatre in the world.
✚ N24 ✉ Residenzstrasse 1
☎ 22 57 54 Ⓤ U-Bahn Odeonsplatz

DAS SCHLOSS
Great theatre classics are performed all year round in a giant tent on the outskirts of the Olympiapark.
✚ K22 ✉ Ackermannstrasse 77 ☎ 300 30 13 🚌 Bus 33

DEUTSCHES THEATER
The number-one venue for musicals, revues and ballets.
✚ N23
✉ Schwanthalerstrasse 13
☎ 552 34 360 Ⓤ U- or S-Bahn Karlsplatz

GASTEIG
Home of the Munich Philharmonic Orchestra and the city's main cultural centre (see panel opposite).
✚ 025 ✉ Rosenheimerstrasse 5 ☎ 48 09 80 Ⓢ S-Bahn Rosenheimer Platz

HERKULESSAAL
Munich's most impressive concert-hall, in the Residenz.
✚ N24 ✉ Residenzstrasse 1
☎ 29 06 71 Ⓤ U-Bahn Odeonsplatz

HOCHSCHULE FÜR MUSIK
Young up-and-coming musicians from the Music Academy give regular free evening concerts and lunchtime recitals. Telephone for details.
✚ M23 ✉ Arcisstrasse 12
☎ 559 15 75 Ⓤ U-Bahn Königsplatz

KOMÖDIE IM BAYERISCHEN HOF
Sophisticated light comedy is the speciality here.
✚ N23 ✉ Promenadeplatz 6
☎ 29 28 10 Ⓤ U- or S-Bahn Karlsplatz

LACH UND SCHIESS-GESELLSCHAFT
Germany's most satirical revues are performed here.
✚ L25 ✉ Ursulastrasse 9
☎ 39 19 97 Ⓤ U-Bahn Münchener Freiheit

MÜNCHNER KAMMERSPIELE
The 'Munich Playhouse' is considered one of Germany's best theatres. Tickets are like gold dust.
✚ N24 ✉ Maximilianstrasse 26 ☎ 23 72 13 28 Ⓤ U- or S-Bahn Marienplatz

MÜNCHNER MARIONETTEN-THEATER
A delightful puppet theatre with shows for children in the afternoons and marionette opera for adults in the evenings.
✚ 023 ✉ Blumenstrasse 29
☎ 26 57 12 Ⓤ U-Bahn Sendlinger Tor

MÜNCHNER THEATER FÜR KINDER
The German language proves no barrier for children in this magical theatre where fairy-tales

come alive. Popular favourites include Pinocchio and Hänsel and Gretel.

✚ M22 ✉ Dachauerstrasse 46 ☎ 59 54 54 Ⓜ U-Bahn Stiglmaierplatz

NATIONALTHEATER (BAVARIAN STATE OPERA)

One of Europe's most respected opera-houses. The opera festival in July is the high point of Munich's cultural year.

✚ N24 ✉ Max-Joseph-Platz 2 ☎ 21 85 01 Ⓜ U- or S-Bahn Marienplatz

PLATZL THEATERIE

Enjoy a variety show while you dine – music, dancing, magic and comedy and, occasionally, traditional yodellers and Bavarian folk dancing.

✚ N24 ✉ Am Platzl 1 ☎ 23 70 36 66 Ⓜ U- or S-Bahn Marienplatz

PRINZREGENTEN-THEATER

Originally built to emulate the famous Wagner Festspielhaus in Bayreuth in 1900. Today it stages plays, concerts and musicals.

✚ N25 ✉ Prinzregentenplatz 12 ☎ 29 16 14 14 Ⓜ U-Bahn Prinzregentenplatz

RESIDENZTHEATER

A modern theatre performing a broad repertoire of classical and contemporary plays.

✚ N24 ✉ Max-Joseph-Platz 1 ☎ 21 85 19 40 Ⓜ U-Bahn Odeonsplatz

STAATSTHEATER AM GÄRTNERPLATZ

This flourishing theatre claims to be the only municipal light opera-house in the world, with a wide repertoire of operetta, light opera, musicals and ballet.

✚ O24 ✉ Gärtnerplatz 3 ☎ 201 67 67 Ⓜ U-Bahn Fraunhoferstrasse

THEATER BEI HEPPEL & ETTLICH

A relaxed atmosphere and a glass of beer welcome you to this student bar/theatre.

✚ L24 ✉ Kaiserstrasse 67 ☎ 34 93 59 Ⓜ Tram 12, 27

THEATER DER JUGEND

Here the shows appeal to both small children (morning and afternoon performances) and teenagers (evening shows).

✚ L24 ✉ Franz-Joseph-Strasse 47 ☎ 23 72 13 65 Ⓜ U-Bahn Giselastrasse

THEATER IM MARSTALL

Avant-garde theatre and experimental performances by the State Opera and the Residenztheater company.

✚ N24 ✉ Marstallplatz 4 ☎ 21 85 19 40 Ⓜ U-Bahn Odeonsplatz

Gasteig

This modern cultural, educational and conference centre lies at the centre of Munich's music scene, focused on its splendid concert-hall with its much-praised acoustics. There are concerts in the Carl-Orff-Saal and during weekday lunchtimes students of the resident Richard Strauss Conservatory give free recitals in the Kleine Konzertsaal. Gasteig houses Germany's largest city library, and is the venue for the annual Film Festival, along with a full programme of dance, experimental theatre, films and jazz.

SPORT & OUTDOOR ACTIVITIES

PARTICIPANT SPORTS

Football fever

It is hardly surprising that football is Bavaria's most popular sport with FC Bayern München and TSV 1860 München at the top of the German league, and boasting an international player in virtually every position respectively. When playing at home, massive crowds throng the terraces, decked from head to foot in red-and-white (Bayern) or blue-and-white (TSV 1860), regularly filling the Olympic Stadium to its capacity of 70,000.

BOWLING
ISAR-BOWLING

One of Munich's biggest ten-pin bowling alleys, with special 'Moonlight-Disco-Bowling' at weekends.

✚ Q24 ✉ Martin-Luther-Strasse 22 ☎ 692 45 12 Ⓜ U-Bahn Silberhornstrasse

BUNGEE-JUMPING
BUNGEE JUMPING JOCHEN SCHWEIZER

Get a new perspective on Munich, hanging upside-down from a bridge!

✚ Off map to southeast ✉ Bettinastrasse 22 ☎ 606 08 90 Ⓢ S-Bahn Neubiberg

CURLING
OLYMPIA-EISSTADION

This traditional Alpine sport held on Thursday evenings at the Olympic Ice Stadium is exhilarating and fun.

✚ J22 ☎ 30 67 21 50 Ⓜ U-Bahn Olympiazentrum

CYCLING
RADIUS TOURISTIK

Rent a bike at the main station and explore the city with its 1,300km of cycle paths. The tourist office's brochure *Sightseeing by Bike* will help you plan your route.

✚ N22 ✉ Hauptbahnhof (near platform 31) ☎ 59 61 13 Ⓜ U- or S-Bahn Hauptbahnhof

FITNESS
PRINZ

Pump iron with the likes of Boris Becker at Munich's smartest fitness centre.

✚ N26 ✉ Prinzregentenplatz 9 ☎ 470 90 41 Ⓜ U-Bahn Prinzregentenplatz

GOLF
FELDAFING GOLF CLUB

One of the finest golf courses in Europe, overlooking Starnberger See.

✚ Off map to southwest ✉ Feldafing ☎ (08157) 7005 Ⓢ S-Bahn Feldafing

HIKING
DEUTSCHER ALPENVEREIN

This Alpine walkers' club organises walking excursions in the mountains. Why not tackle the nearby Zugspitze, Germany's highest mountain?

✚ N24 ✉ Praterinsel 5 ☎ 235 09 00 🚋 Tram 17, 19

HOT-AIR BALLOONING
BLUE UP

Don't let the name put you off this chance of a lifetime, guaranteeing exceptional views of the Alps.

✚ L23 ✉ Lindenmannstrasse 2, Tutzing ☎ (08158) 13 60 Ⓢ S-Bahn Tutzing

ICE-SKATING
OLYMPIC PARK SKATING RINK

Rent your ice-skates at the door and enjoy this magnificent rink.

✚ J22 ☎ 30 61 32 35 Ⓜ U- or S-Bahn Olympiazentrum

RIDING
REITVEREIN CORONA

Say goodbye to the city and explore the Bavarian countryside on horseback.

⊞ Off map to south
✉ Muttenthalerstrasse 31
☎ 79 80 80 Ⓢ S-Bahn Solln

SKIING
SPORT-SCHECK
It takes an hour by car to the nearest ski slopes; this department store will organise your trip.
⊞ N23 ✉ Sendlingerstrasse 85 ☎ 21 66 12 54 Ⓤ U-Bahn Sendlinger Tor

SWIMMING (INDOOR POOLS)
MÜLLERSCHES VOLKSBAD
Germany's loveliest swimming pool, in the *Jugendstil* style.
⊞ O24 ✉ Rosenheimer Strasse 1 ☎ 23 61 34 29 🚋 Tram 18

SWIMMING (OUTDOOR POOLS)
DANTEBAD
Swimming while it snows is quite an experience at this pool, open all year.
⊞ K21 ✉ Dantestrasse 6 ☎ 15 28 74 🚌 Bus 83, 177

TENNIS
TENNISANLAGEN OLYMPIAPARK
Tennis buffs can enjoy a game here. Booking essential.
⊞ K21 ☎ 30 67 20 50 🚋 Tram 20, 21

WATERSPORTS
AMTLICHES BAYERISCHES REISEBÜRO
Drift along the Isar on a raft in true Bavarian style with music and beer (see panel).
⊞ N22 ✉ Bahnhofplatz 2 ☎ 12 04 1 Ⓤ U- or S-Bahn Hauptbahnhof

MAX SCHROPP
Learn to windsurf on the Starnberger See, or rent a sailing boat to explore this beautiful lake with its Alpine backdrop.
⊞ Off map to south
✉ Seepromenade Boothaus 4, Starnberg ☎ (08151) 162 52 Ⓢ S-Bahn Starnberg

SPECTATOR SPORTS

FOOTBALL
The atmosphere is electric when FC Bayern München or TSV 1860 play their home matches in the Olympic Stadium (see panel opposite).
⊞ K22 ☎ 30 67 0 Ⓤ U-Bahn Olympiazentrum

TENNIS
COMPAQ GRAND SLAM
This annual five-day December tournament has developed into one of the most prestigious and glamorous events in international tennis with one of the biggest sporting cash prizes in the world.
⊞ J22 ✉ Olympiahalle ☎ 95 72 57 14 (ticket office) Ⓤ U-Bahn Olympiazentrum

HORSE RACING
Flat racing is held weekly at the racecourse in Riem from March to November, while trotting races are held in nearby Daglfing (☎ 930 00 10).
⊞ Off map to east ✉ Graf-Lehdorff-Strasse 36 ☎ 90 88 81 Ⓢ S-Bahn Riem

River rafting
One of the most enjoyable boating experiences in Bavaria is a pleasure raft trip (*Gaudiflossenfahrt*) on the River Isar. Boarding at Wolfratshausen, you will drift downstream in a convoy of rafts to the music of a brass band and a steady flow of beer from the barrels on board. The highlight of the afternoon is undoubtedly the waterslide before reaching your destination in Thalkirchen. Great fun.

LUXURY HOTELS

Prices

Expect to pay over DM300 per night for a double room at a luxury hotel.

Crème de la crème

The traditional Vier Jahreszeiten (Four Seasons) hotel is perfectly placed on Munich's most exclusive shopping street and within easy walking distance of most of the main city sights. It was established in the mid-19th century as a guest-house for royalty visiting King Maximilian II and is still used today to accommodate visiting dignitaries. The Walterspiel restaurant is particularly well known for its superb cuisine.

BAYERISCHER HOF

A classic Munich hotel, run by the same family for over 150 years. Its excellent facilities include a roof-garden health centre, swimming pool and several top-class restaurants.

➕ N23 ✉ Promenadeplatz 2–6 ☎ 212 00 Ⓜ U- or S-Bahn Marienplatz

DER KÖNIGSHOF

One of Munich's top hotels, with one of the best restaurants.

➕ N23 ✉ Karlsplatz 25 ☎ 55 13 60 Ⓜ U- or S-Bahn Karlsplatz

EXCELSIOR

Ideally sited in the tranquil pedestrian zone, three minutes' walk from the main station.

➕ N23 ✉ Schützenstrasse 11 ☎ 55 13 70 Ⓜ U- or S-Bahn Hauptbahnhof

HILTON PARK

The Hilton has 960 beds plus outdoor dining, beer garden, indoor pool and business centre, and fantastic views over the English Garden.

➕ M25 ✉ Am Tucherpark 7 ☎ 38 45 0 Ⓜ U-Bahn Giselastrasse 🚌 Bus 54

OPERA

This small, homely hotel, with only 50 beds, is set in a delightful old mansion, with an attractive inner courtyard.

➕ N24 ✉ St-Anna-Strasse 10 ☎ 22 55 33 Ⓜ U-Bahn Lehel

PLATZL

A friendly hotel with 170 traditionally decorated rooms. Top-class facilities include a fitness centre and a beautiful restaurant in a converted mill.

➕ N24 ✉ Sparkassenstrasse 10 ☎ 23 70 30 Ⓜ U- or S-Bahn Marienplatz

PRINZREGENT

Tradition and comfort combine in an elegant, rustic setting at this popular hotel, with 80 rooms and an attractive garden for breakfast and aperitifs.

➕ N25 ✉ Ismaningerstrasse 42-44 ☎ 41 60 50 Ⓜ U-Bahn Max-Weber-Platz

RAFFAEL

Guests at Munich's newest luxury hotel have included Madonna and Prince Charles.

➕ N24 ✉ Neuturmstrasse 1 ☎ 29 09 80 Ⓜ U- or S-Bahn Marienplatz

RESIDENCE

Rent a luxury studio or apartment in this quiet side street in Schwabing.

➕ K24 ✉ Artur-Kutscher-Platz 4 ☎ 38 17 80 Ⓜ U-Bahn Münchener Freiheit

VIER JAHRESZEITEN KEMPINSKI

Munich's 'flagship' hotel, at the heart of Munich (see panel).

➕ N24 ✉ Maximilianstrasse 17 ☎ 21 25 0 Ⓜ U-Bahn Odeonsplatz

MID-RANGE HOTELS

ADMIRAL

This smart Hotel Garni with 50 rooms, near the river and the Deutsches Museum, offers special weekend packages.

✚ 024 ✉ Kohlstrasse 9 ☎ 22 66 41 Ⓢ S-Bahn Isartor

ANGLETERRE

A small, personal hotel, with an excellent buffet breakfast, ideally located for exploring the city centre and Schwabing.

✚ M22 ✉ Dachauerstrasse 91 ☎ 521 63 32 Ⓤ U-Bahn Stiglmaierplatz

BIEDERSTEIN

A small hotel with 45 beds, in a quiet backstreet in Schwabing.

✚ L25 ✉ Keferstrasse 18 ☎ 39 50 72 Ⓤ U-Bahn Münchener Freiheit

CARLTON

Very reasonably priced for its location, a stone's throw from Odeonsplatz, this hotel is a treasured secret for those in the know.

✚ M24 ✉ Fürstenstrasse 12 ☎ 28 20 61 Ⓤ U-Bahn Odeonsplatz.

EXQUISIT

A small, elegant hotel in a secluded side street near Karlsplatz, Marienplatz and the Oktoberfest site.

✚ N23 ✉ Pettenkoferstrasse 3 ☎ 551 99 00 Ⓤ U-Bahn Sendlinger Tor

GÄSTEHAUS ENGLISCHER GARTEN

Book well in advance to stay at this oasis on the edge of the English Garden.

✚ L25 ✉ Liebergesellstrasse 8 ☎ 39 20 34 Ⓤ U-Bahn Münchener Freiheit

HABIS

This hotel faces riverside parkland in Haidhausen, with a cosy wine bar and live piano music at weekends.

✚ N25 ✉ Maria-Theresia-Strasse 2a ☎ 470 50 71 Ⓤ U-Bahn Max-Weber-Platz

INSELMÜHLE

This beautifully renovated, half-timbered corn mill is one of the 'Romantik' chain of hotels. Just out of the centre but worth the extra trip.

✚ J17 ✉ Von-Kahr-Strasse 87 ☎ 810 10 Ⓢ S-Bahn Allach

SPLENDID

A small, exclusive hotel in the city centre. Guests can choose their room from a range of styles including baroque, Louis XIV and Bavarian.

✚ N24 ✉ Maximilianstrasse 54 ☎ 29 66 06 Ⓤ U-Bahn Lehel

TORBRÄU

A well-established, traditional hotel at the heart of Munich's Old Town. Facilities include an Italian restaurant, café and confiserie.

✚ N24 ✉ Tal 41 ☎ 22 50 16 Ⓢ S-Bahn Isartor

Prices

Expect to pay up to DM300 per night for a double room in a mid-range hotel.

Bookings

Wherever you see the following signs – Gasthof, Gasthaus, Gaststätte, Gästehaus, Fremdenzimmer, Pension, Hotel and Ferienwohnungen – you will find accommodation. With over 350 hotels and guest-houses offering more than 37,000 beds, you are spoilt for choice. Be careful to book early though, especially for the summer holiday period and the Oktoberfest. Prices quoted always include service and taxes, and usually breakfast.

85

BUDGET ACCOMMODATION

Prices

Expect to pay up to DM150 for a double room in a budget hotel.

Camping

For really cheap accommodation in Munich, why not bring a tent? There are three campsites in and around Munich. The best one (and the most central) is Camping Thalkirchen (☎ 723 17 07), attractively positioned along the River Isar, with 700 places open from mid-March until the end of October. There is no need to book apart from during the Oktoberfest.

AM MARKT

A traditional hotel, situated on one of the last original old squares near the Viktualienmarket.

✚ N24 ✉ Heiliggeiststrasse 6 ☎ 22 68 44 🚇 U- or S-Bahn Marienplatz

BED AND BREAKFAST

This company organises rooms in private homes and apartments in the city centre and outskirts.

✚ M23 ✉ Augustenstrasse 59 ☎ 523 61 55 🚇 U-Bahn Theresienstrasse

BLAUER BOCK

A comfortable hotel offering homely accommodation and parking facilities in the town centre. Great value.

✚ N23 ✉ Sebastiansplatz 9 ☎ 23 17 80 🚇 U- or S-Bahn Marienplatz

BURG SCHWANECK

A long way from the city centre but it is worth the S-Bahn journey to stay in this youth hostel in a castle overlooking the River Isar. Youth hostel pass required.

✚ Off map to south ✉ Burgweg 4–6, Pullach ☎ 793 06 43 🚇 S-Bahn Pullach

HAUS INTERNATIONAL

Slightly more expensive than the youth hostels but it does not require a pass.

✚ L23 ✉ Elisabethstrasse 87 ☎ 12 00 60 🚇 U-Bahn Hohenzollernplatz

JUGENDHERBERGE MÜNCHEN (MUNICH YOUTH HOSTEL)

Advance booking and a youth hostel pass are essential here.

✚ M21 ✉ Wendl-Dietrich-Strasse 20 ☎ 13 11 56 🚇 U-Bahn Rotkreuzplatz

MITWOHNZENTRALE

Useful for longer stays in Munich, the Mitwohnzentrale will arrange apartment accommodation for you for a small fee.

✚ L23 ✉ Georgenstrasse 45 ☎ 271 20 19 🚇 U-Bahn Josephsplatz

PENSION FRANK

A reasonable and popular hotel, situated at the heart of trendy Schwabing. Often used by models in town for photo calls.

✚ M24 ✉ Schellingstrasse 24 ☎ 28 14 51 🚇 U-Bahn Universität

SCHILLERHOF

This cheap, simple, well-run pension is located near the main station.

✚ N23 ✉ Schillerstrasse 21 ☎ 59 42 70 🚇 U- or S-Bahn Hauptbahnhof

STEFANIE

A clean, friendly pension in the popular university district, not far from the Neue and the Alte Pinakothek.

✚ M24 ✉ Türkenstrasse 35 ☎ 28 40 31 🚇 U-Bahn Universität

MUNICH
travel facts

ARRIVING & DEPARTING

Before you go

- EU nationals need a valid passport or a national identity card. Citizens of the US, Canada, Australia and New Zealand need a valid passport to stay for up to three months. Other nationals should check visa requirements with the German Embassy.

When to go

- Jun–Aug (warmest); May–Jul (wettest); Dec–Feb (coldest).

Climate

- Average temperatures: January 1°C; April 14°C; July 24°C; October 14°C.

Arriving by air

- Munich's international airport (Flughafen München Franz-Josef-Strauss) is 30km from the city centre.
- ☎ 97 52 13 13 for flight information.
- Taxis from the airport are expensive.
- S-Bahn 8 runs every 20 minutes (24 hours a day) to the city centre, taking 40 minutes to reach the main railway station.
- An airport bus leaves Munich North Terminal every 20 minutes (7:05AM–8:05PM) taking 45 minutes to reach the main railway station.

Arriving by train

- Trains take 18 hours to Munich from Calais or Ostend.
- Munich has good connections with most major European cities.
- Most trains terminate at the main station (Hauptbahnhof).
- The east station (Ostbahnhof) takes regular motorail services from other German stations and from Paris, Budapest, Athens, Istanbul and Rimini.
- Train information from the German National Railway (Deutsche Bahn) is available in the Travel Centre (Reisezentrum) in the main station ✚ N22 ☎ 13 08 23 33.

Arriving by car

- Munich is well served by motorways and the ring road provides easy access to the city centre.
- Follow the clearly marked speed restrictions as fines are harsh.
- Street parking is difficult in the city centre. Use the car parks.

Arriving by bus

- There are frequent coach links with other German cities, starting from the main bus terminal beside the main railway station.

Customs regulations

- No currency restrictions.
- EU nationals are not required to declare items intended for personal use.
- Customs restrictions for non-EU members: 200 cigarettes or 50 cigars or 250g of tobacco; 1 litre of spirits or 2 litres of fortified wine or 3 litres of table wine, plus a further 2 litres of table wine and 50cc of perfume.

Airport tax

- Departure tickets usually include airport tax.

ESSENTIAL FACTS

Travel insurance

- Best to take out a comprehensive policy before you leave home.

Opening hours

- Banks: Mon–Fri 8:30–3:45 (some open Thu until 5:30, many close for lunch).

- Shops: Mon–Fri 9–6, may change to 9–8 (late shopping Thu until 8:30); Sat 9–2 , may change to 9–4 (but 4/6PM on first Sat in the month). Many close for lunch (noon–2).
- Museums and galleries: Tue–Sun 9/10–5. Most close Mon and public holidays. Many are free on Sun.

National holidays

- 1 January, 6 January, Good Friday, Easter Sunday, Easter Monday, 1 May, Ascension Day, Whit Sunday and Whit Monday, Corpus Christi, 15 August, 3 October, 1 November, 3rd/4th week in November:Day of Repentance and Prayer, Christmas Day, 26 December.

Money matters

- The German unit of currency is the *Deutsche Mark* (DM1=100 *Pfennig*)
- Credit cards and travellers' cheques are usually accepted in hotels but in very few shops and restaurants.
- All banks will change foreign notes during normal banking hours.
- Money-changing automats can be found at the airport, the main station and Marienplatz. Banks usually give better exchange rates.
- Exchange offices (*Geldwechsel*) can be found all over Munich. The DVKB exchange office in the main station is open from 6AM–11:30PM.

Etiquette

- Say *Grüss Gott* (good day) and *Auf Wiedersehen* (goodbye) when shopping, *Guten Appetit* (enjoy your meal) when eating, *Entschuldigen Sie* (excuse me) in crowds.
- Never jump lights at pedestrian crossings. Don't walk on cycle paths.

- Dress is generally informal, except for the theatre, opera or nightclubs.
- Although service charges are officially included in bills, tipping is still customary and bills are rounded off.

Women travellers

- Frauenhaus München offers help for women around the clock ☎ 35 48 30.
- Some car parks have well-lit, reserved parking for women only near the main entrance ♿ O25 ✉ Gasteig, Rosenheimerstrasse 5 🕐 8AM–midnight ♿ N23 B Parkhaus am St-Jakobs-Platz, Oberangerasse 35–37 🕐 24 hours

Places of worship

- Roman Catholic: Frauenkirche, Peterskirche, and many others.
- Roman Catholic Services in English: Berchmannskolleg.
- Jewish: contact the Synagogue for details ✉ Reichenbachstrasse 27 ☎ 201 49 60.
- Muslim: Mosque prayer Fri 12:20PM ✉ Wallnerstrasse 1–3 ☎ 32 50 61.
- English services: International Baptist Church, ✉ Holzstrasse 9. Evangelical International Community Church ✉ Enhuberstrasse 10.

Student travellers

- Some museums and theatres offer up to 50 per cent discounts with an International Student ID Card
- A German Rail Youth Pass is available for young people under 26, valid for five, 10 or 15 days. Must be purchased outside Germany.
- For budget accommodation, camping and youth hostels (►86).

Time differences

- Munich is one hour ahead of

Greenwich Mean Time in winter
and two hours ahead in summer.

Toilets

- *Toiletten* are marked *Herren* (men)
and *Damen* (women). *Besetzt* means
occupied, *frei* means vacant. There
is often a small charge.

Electricity

- 220 volts; two-pin sockets. Take
an adaptor with you.

PUBLIC TRANSPORT

- Munich has an excellent (albeit
complicated) public transport
network, with two urban railways,
and a comprehensive network of
bus and tram routes.
- The local transport authority is
the Münchner Verkehrs- und
Tarifverbund (MVV) ✚ N24
✉ Thierschstrasse 2 ☎ 23 80 30

Types of ticket

- The MVV network is divided into
fare zones. Prices are based on the
number of zones required to
complete the trip. For most sightseeing you will remain in the
Innenraum (interior area – marked
blue on station maps). To travel
further you need a ticket valid for
the *Gesamtnetz* (total network).
- Before boarding a train, you must
put your ticket in the blue punch-
ing-machine (*Entwerter*) on the
platform to validate it. On buses
and trams you must immediately
stamp your ticket upon boarding.
- Travelling without a valid ticket
can result in a heavy fine.
- *Kurzstrecken*: 'short trip' single
tickets can be bought for journeys
covering only four stops; two may
be U- or S-Bahn stops. A trip must
not last more than one hour and
can only be used in one direction.
- *Streifenkarte*: a strip of tickets. For

each journey, stamp the appropriate number of strips. A 'short trip'
is one strip. More than two U- or
S-Bahn stops within one zone is
two strips. If you are travelling
outside the blue *Innenraum* zone,
a notice shows how many strips
you need to punch.
- *Einzelfahrkarte*: single tickets can
be bought covering any number of
zones, but a *Streifenkarte* usually
works out cheaper.
- *Tageskarte*: one day's unlimited
travel from 9AM until 6AM the following day. Purchase either a
Single-Tages-Karte for one person,
or a *Partner-Tages-Karte* for up to
five people (maximum two adults).
- *Stammkarte*: a personalised pass
with a weekly ticket (*Wertmarke*) is
available from the MVV office at
the main station. Bring your passport and photos. It is cheaper than
a series of day passes.

Discounts

- Severely disabled people with a
green/orange permit are entitled
to travel free on MVV transport.
- Children under four travel free.
- Children aged four to 14 travel at
reduced fares.
- Summer special offers include a
Kombikarte combining train travel
with trips on excursion steamers
on the Starnberger See and
Ammersee.

The U- and S-Bahn

- U-Bahn (underground) and S-
Bahn (suburban trains) provide a
regular service within a 40km
radius of the city centre. Routes
are referred to by their final stop.
- Underground trains run every 5 or
10 minutes from about 5AM–1AM.
- Tickets are available from auto-
matic ticket machines at stations,
MVV sales points in many stations
or in newspaper shops.

- Most U- and S-Bahn stations have facilities for the disabled.
- Smoking is banned on trains and in the stations.
- Bicycles may be taken on the trains all day Sat, Sun and public holidays; on weekdays not at rush hour (6–8:30AM, 3–6:30PM).

Buses

- Single tickets can be bought from the driver (with small change only). Multiple tickets, also valid for U- and S-Bahn, can be bought from vending machines at train stations, but not from the driver.
- Seven late-night bus lines and three tram lines operate between the centre and the outer suburbs once an hour from 1AM–4AM.

Trams

- Ticket procedures are the same as buses. Some trams have ticket-vending machines on board.
- Scenic routes : trams 18, 19, 20,21 and 27 operate around the old town; tram 20 goes to the English Garden; tram 27 is useful for exploring Schwabing.
- Tram routes are numbered and the tram has a destination board.

Where to get maps and timetables

- MVV station ticket offices and tourist information centres supply free maps and information.
- The MVV publishes a map with details of facilities for the disabled (ramps, lifts, etc.).

Taxis

- Taxis are cream-coloured; stands throughout the city.
- They are not particularly cheap; small surcharge for luggage.
- Car hire: Hertz ☎ 550 22 56
- Chauffeur service: Sixt ☎ 22 28 29

MEDIA & COMMUNICATION

Telephones

- Coin/phonecard telephones are cheaper than hotel telephones. Phonecards can be bought at post offices and newsagents.
- Make long-distance calls from boxes marked International or from telephones in post offices.
- Cheap rate is between 6PM and 8AM on weekdays; all day at weekends.
- National enquiries 011 88.
- International enquiries 00 118.
- The code for Munich from abroad is 89.
- To phone home from Munich, dial 00 followed by your own country code (UK 44, Ireland 353, USA and Canada 1, Australia 61, New Zealand 64), then the number.

Post offices

- Main post office is opposite the railway station ✉ Bahnhofplatz 1 🕐 Mon–Fri 6AM–10PM, weekends and holidays 7AM–10PM.
- Most other post offices are open Mon–Fri 8AM–noon, 3–6PM; Sat 8AM–noon.
- Post boxes are bright yellow and clearly marked 'Munich' and 'other places' (*Andere Orte*).
- Cost for standard letter: European Union DM1; USA, Australia and New Zealand DM3.
- Postcard costs: EU 80 pfennigs; outside the EU DM2.

Newspapers and magazines

- Bavaria's leading daily paper, *Süddeutsche Zeitung*, is published in Munich.
- Munich has several local dailies – *Münchner Abendzeitung*, *tz* and *Bild-Zeitung*, mostly sold from newspaper boxes on street corners.

- There are no local English-language newspapers, but an English-language listings magazine, *Munich Found*, is available.

Radio and television

- Münchners have access to around 20 TV channels, the main ones being ARD, ZDF, SAT 1, RTL and Bayerisches Fernsehen.
- Satellite and cable channels include CNN, an English-language sports channel, MTV, SKY.
- BBC World Service Radio is available on 15070 kHz (daytime), 9410 kHz (evenings).

International newsagents

- Sussmann's Internationale Presse ✉ Hauptbahnhof ☎ 55 117 17 🕐 Daily 7AM–10:45PM.

EMERGENCIES

Sensible precautions

- Munich is one of the safer European cities, but tourists should remain on their guard.
- At night, avoid poorly lit areas and the seedy red-light district behind the main railway station.

Lost property

- Municipal lost property office: ✉ Arnulfstrasse 31 🕐 Mon–Fri 8:30–12 Tue also 2–5 ☎ 12 40 80
- U-Bahn, trams and buses: Fundamt ✉ Arnulfstrasse 31 🕐 Mon–Fri 8:30–12 ☎ 12 40 80
- S-Bahn: Fundstelle ✉ Ostbahnhof 🕐 Mon–Fri 8–5:45, Sat 8–11:45 ☎ 13 08 409
- For items left on Deutsche Bahn trains: Fundbüro der Bundesbahn ✉ Hauptbahnhof, opposite platform 26 🕐 Daily 6:30AM–11:30PM ☎ 13 08 66-64

Medical treatment

- Travel insurance is advisable.
- EU visitors with a valid form E111 (obtainable from main post offices in your native country) can obtain free or reduced-cost emergency medical treatment.
- A list of English-speaking doctors is available at the British and US Consulates.

Medicines and pharmacies

- Take any specially prescribed medicines with you.
- Every neighbourhood has a 24-hour pharmacy (*Apotheke*). Look for the address of that night's 24-hour *Apotheke* in the window.
- International pharmacies have staff who speak different languages. Try Bahnhof-Apotheke ✚ N22 ✉ Bahnhofplatz 2 ☎ 59 41 19) or Internationale Ludwigs-Apotheke ✚ N23 ✉ Neuhauserstrasse 11 ☎ 260 30 21 during shop opening hours.

Emergency phone numbers

- Police ☎ 110
- Fire ☎ 112
- Ambulance ☎ 110 and 112
- Pharmacy emergency service ☎ 59 44 75
- Medical emergency service ☎ 55 77 55
- Dental emergency service ☎ 723 30 93
- Poisons emergency service ☎ 140 22 11
- Rape Hotline ☎ 76 37 37
- Breakdown Service ☎ 01802/22 22 22.

Embassies and consulates in Munich

- USA ✉ Königinstrasse 5 ☎ 288 80
- UK ✉ Bürkleinstrasse 10 ☎ 211 090
- Canada ✉ Tal 29 ☎ 29 06 30

TOURIST OFFICES

Tourist information offices

- Fremdenverkehrsamt München,
  ✉ Sendlingerstrasse 1
  🕐 Mon–Thu 9–3, Fri 9–12:30,
  ☎ 233 0300
- Hauptbahnhof ☎ 233 30256
  🕐 Mon–Sat 9–9, Sun 11–7
- Airport ☎ 97 59 28 15
  🕐 Mon–Sat 8:30–10, Sun and
  holidays 1–9.

German National Tourist Organisation offices

- UK ✉ 65 Curzon Street, London
  W1Y 7PE ☎ 0171 495 0081
  (Mon–Fri 10–noon, 2–4) or
  0891–600 100 (recorded message)
- USA ✉ 122 East 42nd Street,
  New York, NY 10168 ☎ (212)
  661 7200.

LANGUAGE

yes ja
no nein
please bitte
thank you danke
hello Grüss Gott
good morning guten Morgen
good evening guten Abend
good night gute Nacht
goodbye auf Wiedersehen
excuse me please entschuldigen Sie
  bitte
do you speak English? sprechen Sie
  Englisch?
I don't speak German ich spreche
  kein Deutsch
I don't understand ich verstehe nicht
today heute
yesterday gestern
tomorrow morgen
small klein
large gross
cold kalt
hot warm
good gut

menu die Speisekarte
breakfast das Frühstück
lunch das Mittagessen
dinner das Abendessen
white wine der Weisswein
red wine der Rotwein
beer das Bier
bread das Brot
milk die Milch
sugar der Zucker
water das Wasser
bill die Rechnung
room das Zimmer
on the right rechts
on the left links
straight on geradeaus
open offen
closed geschlossen
near nahe
far weit
how much does it cost? wieviel
  kostet es?
expensive teuer
cheap billig
Where are the toilets? Wo sind die
  Toiletten?
Where's the bank? Wo ist die Bank?
station der Bahnhof
airport der Flughafen
luggage das Gepäck
post office das Postamt
chemist die Apotheke
police die Polizei
hospital das Krankenhaus
doctor der Arzt

**Monday, Tuesday, Wednesday,
Thursday, Friday, Saturday
Sunday** Montag, Dienstag,
Mittwoch, Donnerstag, Freitag,
Samstag, Sonntag

1	eins	**9**	neun
2	zwei	**10**	zehn
3	drei	**11**	elf
4	vier	**12**	zwölf
5	fünf	**20**	zwanzig
6	sechs	**50**	fünfzig
7	sieben	**100**	hundert
8	acht		

INDEX

CityPack
Munich

Written by Teresa Fisher
Edited, designed and produced by
  AA Publishing

Maps © The Automobile Association 1997
Fold-out map © RV Reise- und Verkehrsverlag Munich · Stuttgart
  © Cartography: GeoData

Distributed in the United Kingdom by AA Publishing, Norfolk House, Priestley Road, Basingstoke, Hampshire, RG24 9NY.

The contents of this publication are believed correct at the time of printing. Nevertheless, the publishers cannot be held responsible for any errors or omissions or for changes in the details given in this guide or for the consequences of any reliance on the information provided by the same. Assessments of attractions, hotels, restaurants and so forth are based upon the author's own personal experience and, therefore, descriptions given in this guide necessarily contain an element of subjective opinion which may not reflect the publishers' opinion or dictate a reader's own experiences on another occasion.
We have tried to ensure accuracy in this guide, but things do change and we would be grateful if readers would advise us of any inaccuracies they may encounter.

© The Automobile Association 1997

A CIP catalogue record for this book is available from the British Library.

ISBN 0 7495 1429 9

Published by AA Publishing (a trading name of Automobile Association Developments Limited, whose registered office is Norfolk House, Priestley Road, Basingstoke, Hampshire RG24 9NY. Registered number 1878835).

Colour separation by Daylight Colour Art Pte Ltd, Singapore
Printed and bound by Dai Nippon Printing Co (Hong Kong) Ltd.

Acknowledgements

The Author wishes to thank Deutsche B.A., the Hotel Angleterre, the Munich Tourist Office, Michaela Netzer and Emmanuel Vermot for their help.
The Automobile Association wishes to thank the following photographers, libraries and museum for their assistance in the preparation of this book: Bridgeman Art Library, London 32b *The Laundress* by Edgar Degas; Mary Evans Picture Library 12; Teresa Fisher 8, 30, 39a; Edmund Nägele,FRPS 25a; Photo Press/Dr Brucker, 27a; Spectrum Colour Library 20; Toy Museum, Munich 23a, 60.
The remaining photographs are held in the Association's own library (AA Photo Library) and were taken by Clive Sawyer with the exception of pages 21, 53 which were taken by Adrian Baker and pages 7, 18, 23b, 24a, 25b, 26, 27b, 28a, 28b, 29a, 31a, 33b, 34, 35a, 35b, 38, 41a, 41b, 42a, 42b, 44, 47, 49b, 50a, 50b, 52, 55a, 56, 57, 61a, 87b taken by Tony Souter.

Cover photographs

Main picture: Pictures Colour Library   Inset: AA Photo Library (C. Sawyer)

JOINT SERIES EDITORS *Josephine Perry and Rebecca Snelling*
COPY EDITOR *Karen Bird*
VERIFIER *Adi Kraus* INDEXER: *Marie Lorimer*

Titles in the CityPack series

• Atlanta • Bangkok • Berlin • Chicago • Hong Kong • London • Los Angeles •
• Madrid • Montréal • Moscow • Munich • New York • Paris • Prague • Rome •
• San Francisco • Singapore • Sydney • Tokyo • Vienna • Washington •